TRAVELS WITHOUT A DONKEY

Here root and branch together lie
In silence they report
To heedless mortals passing by
Remember time is short

Copied from a gravestone in the old kirkyard at Muthill, near the cathedral ruins—July 16th, 1965.

DAVID TOULMIN

TRAVELS
WITHOUT
A DONKEY

Windscreen Memories
of
Scotland and Northumbria

GOURDAS HOUSE, PUBLISHERS
ABERDEEN
1980

ISBN 0 907301 00 2

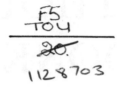

Printed & bound in the United Kingdom
by Clark Constable Ltd., Edinburgh

Contents

Introduction to my Travels   pages ix–xiv

MY JOURNAL FOR THE YEARS

1963	*page*	1
1964		5
1965		9
1966		24
1967		56
1968		83
1969		116
1970		148
1973		152
1974		157
1977		167

Introduction

One of the best things that happened to me in middle-age was learning to drive a car. Formerly I had to make do with a bicycle, mostly on Sunday afternoons from the various farms on which I worked, but seldom getting beyond the parish boundaries, until I removed to another farm, thus widening my radius by a few parishes, but seldom if ever reaching a neighbouring county.

It was common in those days to live your entire life in the parish of your birth, to live and die within the restricting compass of a few square miles, without ever being beyond the border of the next shire. Living in Aberdeenshire your greatest Mecca (or Jerusalem) was to visit its capital city, Aberdeen, and to go beyond that you were almost a foreigner. Those privileged to go further afield were of the upper classes, teachers, bankers or civil servants, or those employed by the military, while the farm servant stagnated in his own mire. The double journey to the city, by train or bus, usually took about four hours, mostly on the Term Day twice a year by the farm workers, and those that were nearer the city cycled it. Even that was a privilege, for mostly on Term or Feeing Market days you were preoccupied too much in searching for a job or flitting to the next farm, and gallivanting the country-side was the least of your priorities, especially if you were a married man.

My own father and Jane's mother (my mother-in-law) were never beyond Aberdeen, because they lived and died in an age before the motor-car became an accessory of the farm worker. On the other hand my mother and Jane's father lived to riper age, when their married families (including myself) had procured a motor-car, and they were enabled to travel further and see more ferlies. In their own youth they didn't even have bicycles and walked everywhere, unless they lived by the railway line, until the days when the motor-bus came by the end of the farm road and opened up the countryside. Before that country people walked tremendous distances, across whole parishes, even at week-ends, from a place of work to their homes and back again, while others travelled by canal barge or stage coach to Aberdeen, or even on horseback, with an occasional outing by horse cart for the whole family at the sea-side, or to the school picnic.

I was a little more fortunate in being born in the age of the steam train, the puffing-billie and the traction engine, even though motor-buses were still charabancs with canvas hoods and solid rubber tyres and hard makeshift seats; and they ran mostly on Sundays or public holidays, the latter never allowed to farm workers. When I left school the only advantage I had over my father was that after my first six-months' fee I could afford a bicycle, at least a second-hand one, whereas for years he had to walk from the farm where he worked to his home at week-ends for a change of underclothes, and of course walk back again.

In my own youth the horse and the bicycle still predominated, and the motor-car was still the prerogative of the rich and privileged, which didn't even include the farmers, and the working man had to make do with his bicycle. But the social structure has changed dramatically, so that nowadays, and even with the farmers, I can park my car alongside that of the business executive or the manicured civil servant and pay my admission ticket to look at the stately homes of the despairing rich, who are only too glad to have my donation which will entitle me to ramble through their private bedrooms and exclusively furnished drawing-rooms, and will enable them to replace the odd slate in the leaking roof, until the day when the Inland Revenue has reduced them to the indignity of bequeathing the property to the care of the National Trust—grounds and policies where, in my youth, I wouldn't have dared to set foot beyond the gate-keeper's lodge, and the private sign at the entrance, unless I had been looking for employment in the spacious walled gardens that are now a wilderness. Not mind you that I despise the rich, for in many ways the best of them have beautified the countryside and left us a rural tradition to be proud of, and have done a service to agriculture which has survived with great benefits into the days of mechanisation; what with their wide and well-drained fields, solid dykes and sheltering tree belts, though some of the more expansive minded of the "Golden Handshake" farmers have seen fit to bury the dykes with bulldozer to enlarge the fields still further, in the wider sense of combine harvesting, and have cut down the ornamental trees and rebuilt the laird's steadings, while the tourists still flock to the Big House.

But I am not personally responsible for the fluctuations of fortune, or for the economic changes in our society; a revolutionary phenomenon which has raised the standard of living for the working classes and widened the scope of their geographical outlook, to say nothing of the social consciousness which has raised their eyes from the feudal grindstone to behold the wonders of a fuller life, enhanced considerably by the mobility of the motor-car.

But motoring is expensive; always has been in a comparative scale of earning ability, and only the higher wages and increased overtime has made it possible for the average working man to maintain and run a motor-car. In my own case, as a farm worker, in those days at the lower end of the wages bracket, it was perhaps more difficult than for the union-backed, shop-stewarded industrial workers, some of whom were being paid £40 a week while we had to exist on £10 to £12, with some ancillary benefits.

Our first car, a Hillman Minx, which I bought in 1956, cost us £40, which exhausted our bank account at the local post-office, and by then the car was 22 years old; a "banger" by modern standards, but in such good condition body wise, that had it been preserved it could have been a vintage model. Mechanically it required a lot of oil, almost a pint to the gallon of petrol by the time we got rid of it four years later, but as there were no road tests to be observed I didn't have to worry much about repairs, apart from the odd polish-up and changing of spark plugs and general maintenance. Having owned a motor-bike in 1932, twenty-four years earlier, I didn't have to sit a driving test, and scarcely capable of getting the thing into top gear, especially with a non-synchromesh gear-box, which compelled me to practice the double-declutch method of contemporary bus and heavy-duty vehicle drivers—despite this, and barely responsible for taking hold of the steering wheel, and with only a smattering of the Highway Code, I was immediately issued with a fully qualified driving licence for all groups, which in those days included a public service vehicle, a traction engine or a crane transporter, and the letter confirming my privilege was signed with the compliments of the then reigning Town Clerk for the county.

I was among the first half-dozen farm workers in the parish to own a motor-car, despite the fact that I am not in the least mechanically minded. Some could afford it but were afraid they would be offending their employers by purchasing a motor-car, regarding it as a sort of insubordination or a challenge to his authority or position on the social ladder, a supposition that could have been dispelled with a glance at the difference between the condition and age of the worker's car in comparison to the elegance of the car belonging to his employer. In my own case the farmer was most compromising, and he even offered me garage space for it at the steading, there being no such accommodation at the cottar house. The thing that annoyed him most I think was my working for other farmers in the evenings for extra cash to run the motor-car, since he had no need for us on overtime at the home farm, not at the time, but being a cottar you were practically owned by your employer, and he jealously guarded your efforts for his own benefit.

In 1956 the traffic on the roads was thin by modern standards, and within a month, with the aid of my sons, two of whom already had a driving licence, I had mastered the knack of handling the car, even to the extent of earning the family nick-name of Stirling Moss, which I hardly considered to my credit in the circumstances. Of course I had the odd mischanter and narrow escape, like the time I missed my gear when changing down on a steep hill, for you had to be very slick at this when double-declutching, and the car began to run backwards, until I secured the hand-brake, when Jane jumped out and could scarcely be persuaded to sit beside me again. But the lure of new horizons beckoned us, and with no further mishaps Jane eventually gained confidence in my capabilities, or a trust in my guardian angel, and since then we have motored the length and breadth of Scotland, even venturing across the border into England, and our adventures and honeymooning is the subject of this little book, a reminder of the eloquent joy such travelling has brought to us in the autumn of our lives together.

We had been brought up on bicycles, went courting on bicycles, cycled to our own wedding on bicycles, gone to work on bicycles, to markets, fairs, concerts and cinemas, dances and auction sales, visited relations; everywhere on bicycles, which perhaps accounts for our excellent constitutional health in our later years. Yet we feel we have earned the right to indulge in a luxury which was denied us in the days of our youth, but well aware, considering the tremendous mileage we have covered over the years that both of us must have charmed lives.

The first of our car journeys were confined to little more than the extent of my former cycle runs, the real difference being that Jane could accompany me, with our school-age son in the back-seat, with a neighbour boy to keep him company, whereas in former days Jane would have been obliged to stay at home and look after him, while I scoured the hills with my bicycle. Now she could share the joys of new discoveries, a pleasant diversion from the kitchen sink; moreso when our three sons grew up and could take care of themselves or got married and we could go anywhere we pleased, even to visit our grandchildren. Since then we have picnicked all over Scotland and slept in many byways, listening to the music of trebling waters; awakening to watch the veils of mist on silent hills, transmitting a strange delight in our hearts that we have lived to share such treasures.

And, for all the defects and imperfections of the motor-car, or what is derided as "the joys of motoring" we have found the said vehicle infinitely more useful and reliable and less temperamental than R. L. Stevenson's donkey while travelling in the Cevennes of south-eastern France. Whereas "Modestine" would scarcely condescend to carry his water jar, much less his bedding, even at a pace despicably slower than walking, despite conscientious application of the switch on the part of the slogging author, we were enabled, by utilising the spacious boot of our long-life Vauxhall Viva (which replaced the Hillman and three other vehicles) to transport our baggage and camping gear from John o' Groats to Hadrian's Wall in Northumbria, and apart from a broken silencer, we endured no eccentricities or complaints whatever from our mechanical beast of burden.

Throughout the years I have diligently kept a diary, jotting down the regional discoveries of my cycle runs, a horizon which was widened immeasurably with the acquisition of a motor-car. From passages like "Today I cycled to the beautiful St. Matthew's Chapel at Oldmeldrum", or "This afternoon I leaned over the dyke and looked at the gravestones in the old churchyard at Newmachar", places within eight or ten miles of home, I have since been enabled to quote that Jane and I have literally prayed in churches from Canisby in Caithness to Mochrum in Galloway, and that we have looked at castles from Dunbeath in Sutherland to Culzean in Ayrshire, and have walked in consecrated abbeys from Fortrose to Dundrennan; that we have looked through stained glass from Dunfermline and Dunblane to Inverness and Tain, and that we have gone on pilgrimage to battlefields from Culloden to Bannockburn and Flodden, none of which we could have accomplished without the motor-car, and certainly not enjoyed with the same freedom and privilege by any other means of transport.

Holidays with pay were another innovation which greatly extended our horizons, whereby we were enabled to stay away for a week or a fortnight, compared with the one-day holiday of the bicycle era. Nowadays of course even working people can go abroad for their holidays by aeroplane, but so far we have confined ourselves to Scotland, and we are not likely to take to the air in our old age, though I do enjoy the occasional rail journey, and I wouldn't mind a sea cruise to places like Greece and ancient Rome, or to the lands of the Bible. Travel widens the scope of one's intelligence, and I hate to think how narrow our thinking would have been without the motor-car; even considering television, though both of these inventions have considerably broadened the thinking sphere of the working-classes compared with that of our immediate ancestors, when a countryman might endure for a lifetime without a glimpse of the sea, or when a city dweller might exist perenially almost unaware of the scenic beauty of his native countryside.

1963

But now I must go back to 1963, some seven years after we had purchased our first motor-car, and were now in possession of an A30 Austin Countryman, with side windows and a chrome grill, which I had purchased from a local dealer for £100, and which served us faithfully for three years with only one singular mishap, namely a broken fanbelt. Never even a tyre puncture that I can remember, though I suppose I had changed the spark plugs from time to time and adjusted the points, or had my son do it for me, seeing he is something of a mechanic.

Looking at my journal for 1963 I find that on July 18th, which was a Thursday, I wrote the following: Cutting thistles with scythe on old pasture. The cows were grazing around us, mostly Ayrshires, with a sprinkling of black and white Friesians. The sun was bright and warm in the morning, but there had been rain overnight and it brought out a perfume from the white clover, a sweet drowsy scent as one feels at haymaking, which attracted the bees, though most of them settled in the buttercups. There were bluebells on the dykes that shook in the wind, a carillon of noiseless ecstasy. Truly a land flowing in milk and honey.

My thoughts were full of the sad sweet sickness of bygone adversities, my head bowed in thankfulness that I still survived to reflect on old lost battles that Time had turned almost to victories.

So much for my working life, though the environment wasn't always so pleasant. Next month, on August 7th, a typical car run to the city; I took my wife in the car to Aberdeen. It was raining. I left her at Aunt Vera's (her sister) and went myself to the Public Library. There I read extracts from the diaries of Katherine Mansfield and Fred Bason. This last writer was most interesting to me because he has lived with my own generation. Read and took a few notes for about 2½ hours. I would have stayed longer but I was craving for a smoke. My bladder also was distended and study isn't easy on an empty stomach.

The sun was shining on the city when I came out, sparkling like crystal on the wet buildings. The trees made a lovely shade of green against the dappled blue of the breaking sky. I couldn't wish for heaven to be better than this, nor could I hope for the angels to be prettier than the girls of Aberdeen. If beauty of face and grace of figure were all the virtues required of an actress they could be picked like wild flowers, almost at random in the Silver City.

I feel self-conscious in my new suit. The texture is a lighter shade than I am accustomed to and I feel somewhat conspicuous on the sidewalks. But I shall get used to it. After all I wanted a brighter holiday suit and I must appreciate my own decision. I am not so easily fitted with an off-the-hook ready-to-wear suit nowadays. I am heavier: 12 st. 2 lbs. and I have a bigger tummy, which has to be buttoned in; middle-age spread I suppose and a somewhat easier job, for I have given up cattle tending and am now employed on general outside duties as an "orraman", sometimes on a tractor—and I was 50 last month.

So now you have me in the picture, vain and conceited if you chose to consider me (though I do not mean to be) and would prefer otherwise in your judgement, at work and at play, but always devoted to literature in providing a comprehensive record of our travels on holiday over a period of years. We have made previous excursions by car and by rail of which I made no account; not until 1963, where I find that on August 7th we motored, Jane and I, some 226 miles (double journey) on seven gallons of petrol to Culloden Moor, where we looked around the graves of the Highland clans and went into the small museum on the battlefield. In 1773, 27 years after the battle, Dr. Johnson stood on the moor and remarked: "They (meaning the Hanoverians I presume) have made a desert here and they have called it peace". We also made an excursion to the pre-historic burial cairns and the standing stones at nearby Clava, in the Valley of the Kings, where the great men of the Neolithic Ages were buried, and it seemed as if the sky still wept over them, because it rained most of the time we were in the area.

So much has been written about Culloden and so many stories told that it ill behoves me to harrow on sprouted grain. My favourite is the one quoted by H. V. Morton in his book

IN SEARCH OF SCOTLAND, concerning the death of Fraser of Inverallochy (Cairnbulg) in my native Buchan. "When the Royalist army swept over the field stabbing the dying, one man was seen leaning against the dyke wall, sick from wounds. He was Fraser of Inverallochy. General Hawley saw him and shouted:

'To whom do you belong?'

'To the Prince,' replied Fraser.

'Shoot that dog!' said Hawley to an A.D.C.

'My commission is at your disposal,' replied the young officer, 'but I will not shoot him.'

'Then a trooper will do so,' said Hawley.

Fraser was shot.

The young officer was Wolfe, afterwards the hero of Quebec. There was a tradition in the Highlands that when he lay dying on the Heights of Abraham it was into the arms of Fraser of Lovat that he fell."

Then there was Dr. Johnson's meeting with Flora Macdonald, related to us by his indefatigable biographer, James Boswell, in his JOURNAL OF A TOUR TO THE HEBRIDES. "She was a little woman, of a mild and genteel appearance, mighty soft and well-bred. To see Mr. Samuel Johnson salute Miss Flora Macdonald was a wonderful romantic scene to me. . . . We had as genteel a supper as one could wish to see, in particular an excellent roasted turkey, porter to drink at table, and after supper claret and punch. But what I admired was the perfect ease with which everything went on."

> Better lo'ed you'll never be.
> Will ye no come back again?

What a great many people do not know is that Bonnie Prince Charlie (a master of disguise) DID come back again, four years after Culloden, in 1750, and his presence was noted in London. Just off the Strand in London, not far from the church of St. Clement Dane's, round the corner in Essex Street, there is a plaque on the wall of a house, one-time home of Lady Anne Primrose, who sheltered the Prince during his five-day visit to the city.

The blue and white plaque was erected by the London County Council at the behest of Lord Amulree.

3

Lady Anne Primrose threw a party, for whatever purpose we do not know, but the Prince appeared suddenly unannounced in the drawing-room, accompanied by Colonel Brett. The Lady Anne, who was playing cards, got such a fright when she saw the Prince that she dropped them in her lap. Apparently he had not been invited, and was supposed to remain out of sight, and his sudden appearance startled her.

Prince Charles had crossed over from France to test the rumoured revival of Jacobite feeling four years after the rout at Culloden.

Providing a lodging for the Prince in Essex Street was a courageous but ignoble venture by Lady Anne, and her apprehension mounted daily because of the carelessness of her Royal guest in concealing his presence from the public gaze. He thought nothing of wandering through St. James's Park and the Mall in broad daylight. He even went to the Tower of London to examine the fortifications, perhaps with a hazy dream of having another go.

On the fifth day of his stay the Prince took his hostess for a walk in Hyde Park, where they encountered someone who instantly recognised him as the Stuart Pretender. That was enough for Lady Anne. She was so upset that she procured a boat that very night and despatched His Royal Highness back to France.

He never came again, but during the visit he attended a church in the Strand and renounced his Roman Catholic faith for that of the Church of England.

Two things happened to us on our drive to Culloden. On the outward journey, just beyond Cock Bridge, on the mountain road to Tomintoul, I overheated a piston and had to wait until the car cooled. Our son Jack had just fitted the new piston in our Hillman Minx (Reg. No. CUH 600) but forgot to tell me to moderate my speed until it was bedded, like the manner of a new car. On the way back, checking the water, in case of overheating, I forgot to replace the radiator cap—you just can't win.

4

1964

On the first run of the year, I drove 80 miles with Jane in the car. We stopped at the monolith which indicates the site of the battle of Corrichie in 1562. It is said that Mary Queen of Scots watched this battle from a boulder on the Hill of Fare overlooking the moor, now known as the Queen's Chair and marked on the maps. There is also a spring nearby named Queen Mary's Well, where she is supposed to have refreshed herself. To the west of the battleground, at the rear of Craigmyle House, nearer Torphins, there is a huge gnarled tree, lichened with age, known as the Darnley Ash, and traditionally known to have been planted by the Scots Queen to commemorate her victory. But while the hill walkers drink from the Queen's well and sit in her rocky chair historians will tell you that the Queen never left Aberdeen on the day of the battle, but waited patiently for reports. Others give you worse tidings: that not only did she witness the orgy of kilted Highlanders hacking each other to pieces on her behalf, but that the day after the battle, in the Castlegate of Aberdeen, she watched the public execution of the clan chiefs of Huntly who were her opponents. No wonder she faced her own death with such callous indifference, though I suppose it could still be called courage; a molten courage, beaten out as a ploughshare on the anvil of life. And even though she didn't watch the battle, surely it was a stigma on her conscience that she was the prime cause of it, between the Protestant and Roman Catholic factions in Scotland. Her skin was so transparent you could see the red burgundy in her throat when she swallowed it—like blood.

The battle of Corrichie was fought between the Protestant Earl of Moray, Lord James Stuart, half-brother to the Queen, and the pro-Catholic Earl of Huntly, who died in the fray from a stroke when he fell from his horse. The Earl of Moray was victorious, and next day, Sir John Gordon, son of the Earl of Huntly, and presumptuous Catholic suitor of the Queen, herself a Catholic, was one of the six Lords beheaded in the Castlegate.

Mourne ye Highlands and Mourne ye Lowlands,
   I trow ye hae muckle need,
For the bonnie burn o' Corrichie
   Has run this day wi' bleed.

I wis our Quine had better friends,
   I wis our countrie better peace;
I wis our lords would na discord;
   I wis our wars at hame may cease.

The obelisk was erected by the Deeside Field Club in 1952 and stands close by the roadside (B977) to Lumphanan at the fourteenth milestone from Aberdeen. Just beyond Lumphanan I stopped the car on the Perkhill to look at the spot where Macbeth was slain by Macduff in 1057, despite Macbeth's assurance by the witches that he couldn't be killed by man born of woman. "But swords I smile at, weapons laugh to scorn, brandish'd by man that's of a woman born." A circle of trees enclosing a cairn of stones marks the site, but it has been said that Macbeth was buried with the Scottish Kings at Iona. Bones were excavated from a burial chamber in the cairn at Lumphanan but reports say they got scant attention from the experts, which is rather a pity because their findings may have provided the elusive fragment in the jig-saw of Macbeth's history, so much disarranged by Shakespeare and legend. Now we don't even know if the head was missing from the skeleton, which might have helped, for you may remember that Macduff carried it on his pike to Malcolm.

This is a far cry from Stratford-on-Avon and the London stage beloved by the students of Shakespeare, and for their sakes as well as my own I like to think that Macbeth still lies within the cairn, mouldering in silent dust. But he wasn't slain at Dunsinane as Shakespeare would have us believe. After the battle he became a fugitive and two years elapsed (some say four) before Malcolm and Macduff caught up with him on Deeside. Legend has it that a broken chimney led his pursuers to Macbeth's last hiding place. Reports got round that he was hiding in a hovel with a fallen chimney. "The lum's fa'n in", somebody said in the doric, and thus the village got its name:

6

Lumphanan, from "Lum-fan-in". And since the scholars of Gaelic are undecided about the origin of the name, giving it as Lanfanan or Lunfanan, with no definite meaning, except "The enclosure by the fair stream", which could describe several villages hereabouts, we may assume that the theory of Macbeth's hiding place is correct.*

Macbeth's full name was Macbeathad MacFinlegh, from his father's surname Finlegh, and I believe that our modern Finlay or Findlay may derive from this source, and that families of that name may be descendants of the followers of Macbeth, who may have adopted his name. So come all ye Findlay exiles and raise your banners at Lumphanan, where the Thane of Glamis and Cawdor still sleeps. 'All hail, Macbeth! that shalt be king hereafter."

After the death of Macbeth his followers succeeded in putting his nephew (or step-son) Lulach on the throne of Scotland for some months. But Malcolm defeated Lulach at Essie, in Strathbogie, on a wintry April day, 1057, and was crowned at Scone three weeks later. To be exact I would say that Lulach reigned (in name anyway) for five months, from the death of his step-father or uncle (Macbeth) on December 5th, 1056, until his own defeat by Malcolm the following spring, April 3rd, 1057.

But take heart all ye Findlays, for the very fact that Macbeth's compatriots tried to put one of his kin on the throne at all might suggest that he wasn't such a bad character as has been said of him, and indeed I have read somewhere that he quelled many factions in Caledonia, and for seven inglorious years brought peace and order and plenty to our barbarous fore-fathers. If he was a tyrant maybe that was what Scotland required at the time; a firm hand to whip the thanes or nobles into obedience. Think what happened three centuries later when Alexander III was killed and the nobles got out of hand.

But enough of Macbeth, for I started up the car again and made for "The Peel of Lumphanan", an earthworks of ditch and mound surrounding a motte or wooden fort of early

---

* "Lumphanan means 'the Cell of St. Finan', one of four disciples of St. Kentigern who proselytised here in the seventh century." Cuthbert Graham in A PORTRAIT OF ABERDEEN AND DEESIDE.

antiquity, probably eleventh century. This Durward stronghold was visited by Edward First of England (the Hammer of the Scots) in 1297, 17 years before Bannockburn, and one wonders if Bruce was in his retinue. It is now in the care of the Ministry of Works for Scotland.

1965

May 29th, Saturday

Car run. We had our tea at the old bridge of Potarch, in a layby overlooking the river Dee. Beautiful view through the trees of the sun-sparkled waters leaping towards the bridge. I read from Carlyle while Jane tried on her new shoes she had bought in the city.

We went as far as Tullich, near the fork at Ballater, looking for Picts' houses, but a man working in his garden told me the one nearby was merely a hole in the ground, in the middle of a field, just below the ruined kirk of Tullich, and might have been a whisky still in the old days, and seeing the field was in crop we didn't go near it, though it is still marked in the guide books. He said the Earth House at Culsh, near Tarland, was much more authentic and was recognised and protected by the Ministry of Works. It is sign-posted and close by the roadside at the farm of Culsh, so we went there and crawled into the pre-historic cavern. It proceeds about 60 feet underground in a semi-circle and one can stand upright in the furthest chamber, which is much wider than the entrance. The passage is sturdily built with huge lintel stones of enormous weight across the roof. It is quite dark inside and I cursed myself for not bringing a torch. I had to strike matches to light the way, but they wouldn't burn in the airless atmosphere. Did the Picts really live here? Or was it merely a hiding place in times of stress and danger? Perhaps even a whisky still and a hide-out for freebooters?

This man at Tullich also told me that the small village of Tullich (now almost extinct) was a Royal Burgh long before Ballater existed as a town. He said that Ballater grew up as a railway terminus and that the Royal Family popularised it. He also informed me that the old kirk of Tullich was the original setting for the composition of the famous REEL O' TULLOCH. The story goes that long ago, on a cold snowy Sabbath morning the minister of the parish was late for service. When he eventually arrived he found the congregation dancing among the tombstones to keep themselves warm. They had waited and wearied so long in the cold they could no longer bear the inactivity, so they broke into stamping around in circles which, by the time the minister arrived had evolved into a mad hooching reel, accompanied by the Highland mouth music of the old Gaels and a grog of whisky. The Rev. John Skinner of Longside had the revellers of Tullich in mind when he wrote THE REEL O' TULLOCHGORUM, which Burns said was the best Scotch song Scotland ever saw. My informant confirmed his story by saying he had never managed to trace a manse for the old kirk at Tullich, unless it had been a farmhouse, so the minister may have had a long way to come to the kirk, a desperate journey on a day of blowing snow.

Our next stop was at Rob Roy's cave on the Burn o' Vat, which flows into Loch Kinnord nearby. The loch is a beautiful sheet of water surrounded by birch trees and is reputed to have an artificial island known as a crannog, perhaps a place of refuge in the olden days of marauding Highlanders.

Here we drank more tea from our thermos flasks. Jane tried on her shoes again and stole some flowers (Sweet Williams) from an uninhabited cottage on the roadside. She nearly ruined her old shoes leaping from stone to stone on the Vat Burn, where she came right inside the Vat with me, where only one person at a time can crouch through the opening in the boulders, the water lapping our feet on the polished stones, the cliffs towering sheer overhead, like you were in a barrel (thus the name of Vat, I suppose), with no other escape but the one by which we came, and before us the waterfall, a curtain of cascading water which almost conceals the entrance to the cave. To make an entry one would have to dash through the waterfall, and we were not prepared for such a wetting.

Local tradition says that Rob Roy MacGregor hid himself here, and it is indeed a clever place of concealment. The rock fissure is screened with trees and the gorge is so unexpected in such a tame and meandering stream. But the whole thing is a deception I think, like the statue of Rob Roy at Culter, and I am doubtful if the famous outlaw was ever much in these parts. The real villain of the legend was a freebooter of lesser gallantry, in the name of Gilderoy, but also of the clan MacGregor, who used the Vat, and who also probably leapt from the rock on the Leuchar Burn at Culter, where the statue is, and thus confuting hereditary belief. All the same it is good for the tourist trade, when visitors believe they are in Rob Roy territory.

About a mile further on towards Tarland I stopped the van and noted the stone obelisk erected in 1956 by the Deeside Field Club to mark the site of the Battle of Culblean, fought on the morning of St. Andrew's Day, November 30th, 1335, a battle which brought a turning point in favour of the Scots in the second War of Independence.

From the Culsh Hill above Tarland we had a splendid view of Lochnagar, Lord Byron's Mountain I told Jane, streaked with sunbeams through distant rain clouds, which gave it an aspect as dark and inspiring as the poet had ever seen it.

Thus over the Perkhill again to Lumphanan, where Jane had a choc-ice bar and I smoked a cigarette in the car and admired the magnificent Stothart Memorial Church spire on the wooded hill above the village. And by the way they still have the "Macbeth Arms" here, the name above the hotel in the square. And so home by Torphins and Kingswells by the Lang Stracht through Aberdeen to Formartine.

June 6th, Sunday

We motored to the old Quakers' Graveyard (1680) at Kinmuck, and looked at the old meeting house of the sect, still intact, and the nearby school, now a ruin. It is to be noted here that there are dates but no particulars on the gravestones of the Quakers, merely the name of the interred, buried humbly and undignified in the hopes of a glorious resurrection. We also paid a visit to the old church and graveyard at Keith-Hall, where the present incumbent, Mr. W. Dodd, is a missionary. Thence on to the old ruined kirk and burial ground at Kinkell, once the Roman Catholic citadel of the parish, and where Gilbert of Greenlaw, who was slain at nearby Harlaw (1411) lies buried. The structure is under the care of the Ministry of Works and permission for interment must be arranged with the County Council.

We had our tea in the van on the banks of the Don and I

read from a life of Shelley. Meanwhile, across the river, in a field near Inverurie, a gymkhana was in progress, where 130 ponies and their youthful riders were competing individually in hurdle demonstrations round a wide circle of spectators and their parked cars. A girl with a delightful feminine voice spoke over the microphone and her words came over the water to us in a pleasant tone. There was the serenity of watching a crowd at a distance, where there is a hushed bustling activity with a minimum of noise, and a wonderful feeling of detachment.

And all the time (although we had almost forgotten) the American astronauts Major James McDivitt and Major Edward White were hurtling through space at five miles a second, circling the earth 100 miles up in the spacecraft Gemini 4. Major White "walked" weightlessly in space for 20 minutes during the flight.

June 20th, Sunday

We came by the old House of Rothie (Rothienorman) to see the rhododendrons, but they were spent, hanging their empty heads in the wet, their faded petals on the ground, soiled with the mud. Rothie House is a roofless, ornamented mansion dating from 1862, but now the haunt of ravens and wild birds and a shelter for cattle. So here was I, a working man with my car, looking at the ruinous opulence of nineteenth-century aristocrats; no doubt a graceful home in its day but now a spectacle of wasteful extravagance, built by the lords of commerce from the enslavement of my kind. How times have changed. A bullock was licking the broken gravestone of the late owner: one Jonathan Forbes Leslie, youngest son of John Forbes of Blackford, born February 22nd, 1798, died December, 1877. There was a family crest with a latin inscription above the main entrance SPE EXSPECTO (I wait with hope), with numerous carvings of boars' heads on a shield of stonework.

Architecture has been called frozen music, if your imagination is capable of transmuting it into life. The only time the blind can see is in their dreams, and scientists estimate that 80 per cent of all our dreams are in colour. And I would hasten to add that when we scream in our sleep the sound is stereophonic. So there.

June 26th, Saturday

We attended a garden fete at a country mansion house in aid of funds for the Conservative Party. Admission to grounds 2/6d., entrance to house 1/-.

I spent about 10/- on old gramophone records and a bundle of books at the jumble sale, while Jane had a pair of new sandals (still in the box) for half-a-crown.

There was tug-o'-war, pipe and fife bands, Highland dancing and all manner of sports and children's games. A spatter of rain halted the games and sent everybody under canvas or into the mansion house, at least for a time, until the sun broke through again in fitful bursts of blinding heat.

The gardens and policies of this family have gone completely to seed, one man now doing the work of six in a vast walled garden so like a wilderness. Dissipation or misfortune, I hardly know which has brought this about, but it seemed to me a pity that they should open their gates to advertise their ruin. I can remember when the laird of this estate was in opulence; when no ordinary person would have dared to approach the mansion house, except as a servant, or they would have set the dogs upon him, and now for a shilling (a day's pay for a serf when the family was in its glory) you can peer into their bedrooms and private apartments and marvel at the leather bound volumes in their extensive library. The house is still in good repair and all the farms on the estates are tenanted and have not been sold (which has happened in so many other cases) and is seems that the present laird, aged about 40, might be hitching up his kilt in an effort to retrieve the remnants of the family fortunes for his children.

I was enthralled by their handsome and expensive library on bible commentary, which included the Apocrypha in two gigantic volumes, and the rest of scripture running to eight or ten volumes, beautifully bound in blue material with silver tooling on the spines. I imagine these tomes are for decoration and seldom consulted, and yet, if I lived in such splendour I would glory in having possession of them, and the liberty to turn their silken leaves when the whim suited me. My father was once a cottar on this estate, and to think I lived in ignorance with such knowledge almost at my finger-tips. But lo! "I am no prophet, I am an husbandman; for man taught me to keep cattle from my youth."—Zechariah 13, 5.

July 18th, Sunday

We are just returned, dear Jane and I, from four days out in the open and three nights under the stars. And by now you must know how I yearn to look at ruined castles and historic sites and in this itinerary I was not disappointed. Ruthven Barracks for instance, a roofless structure high on a green knoll, with the Highland town of Kingussie framed in an open portal, the emerald woods and blue hills in the background, where the Redcoats were garrisoned to guard against further Jacobite uprising after the '45.

We walked round the Festival Theatre at Pitlochry (The Theatre in the Hills) and visited the Hydro-Electric power station and the salmon ladder on the river Tummel.

Church lore is another fad I have developed and I went into several sepulchres and read passages of scripture from the minister's bible. I do not do this purely from any religious motive, but mainly for the love of the poetry. In an empty church you are very much alone with a mighty theme; a Peeping-Tom behind the veil of the unfathomable, and you shrink from the responsibility of being God. In this love of His most holy Word I have riches beyond rubies; a gift bestowed upon me richer than gold, and if position in the world were to be judged by spiritual inspiration I would be one of the richest men on earth.

In the evening of our first day abroad I was divinely inspired by the Book of Job in Moffat's translation of the Old Testament: Phrases like "the storehouses of the snow", "the arsenals of the hail", "tilting the pitchers of the sky", "O thou spy upon mankind", seemed to me imagery of the highest poetical fancy, and taken literally from the original Hebrew appears to be more graphic than the similes of the authorised English version of the bible. It certainly gave the Book of Job as a poem more beauty for me than I ever found in the orthodox reading.

Meanwhile I am aflame with an insatiable love of poetry; this language of wine that exhilarates my being. This word music that sets my poor heart aglow: verse or stanza or poetry

14

in prose, that is why I am so very fond of the bible; its lofty cadences, the simple pastoral images, its majestic flowing style. I just want to soak myself in cold print. I just want to absorb clear black type on the blotting pad of memory, like quenching a feverish thirst with a pleasant refreshing drink.

But Abbotsford was my crowning glory. I actually stood, cap in hand, in the book-lined sanctum where part of Scott's Journal and most of the later novels were written. Here I saw the very quill that set my heart on fire, and the small folded spectacles through which Scott undoubtedly peered at his proof sheets; the seals with which he stamped and sealed his letters; his paper-knife, ink-pot, etc., all there, just as he left them, and a mellowing notebook in which he scribbled data. I almost knelt on the floor in my adulation, and I wanted to handle everything I durst not touch, or sit in the great hide-bound chair that was forbidden.

We saw a cast of Scott's head taken immediately after his demise, a face heavy with sorrow and toil that showed no consolation in death.

And I fairly wallowed in the huge oak-panelled library, spacious and beautiful, with a carved ceiling and crystal candelabra, and oriel windows that looked down on green lawns and the flowing Tweed. The library contains 10,000 volumes, mostly bound in leather, behind glass and wire netting, and as many more in the study. When Scott removed a book for reference he replaced it with a wooden block of similar size, so that there should be no misplacement of the tome. Can you believe that such an industrious author could be so methodical? He was also sheriff of the county and attorney at law, a diversion which enforced his stay in Edinburgh for at least six months in the year.

The armoury too, was resplendent, with enough swords and bucklers to equip a Lonach Gathering of the clans, and suits of mail to clad a jousting tournament. Here a tomahawk from Fenimore Cooper, there a gun used by Rob Roy, a cross-bow used at Cressy, the sword of the great Marquis of Montrose, the crucifix held by Mary Queen of Scots at her execution, the keys of Loch Leven Castle, a necklace of human bones, a chalice from Lord Byron (also filled with human bones); instruments of torture, tapestries, pictures, chinaware, porcelain and trinkets gifted to the bard. There were no museums in Scott's day and people brought him their curios for display at Abbotsford.

And I almost forgot to mention all those priceless manuscripts and first editions of Scott's literary progress in the field of letters.

Nor was my wife's interest allowed to flag, for she was greatly taken with the polished wooden floors and the furnishings nearly took her breath away; ornamental and costly, and especially a bureau of Portuguese ebony, which was gifted to the poet by King George IV when he visited Abbotsford. Jane was also fascinated by the hand-painted Chinese wallpaper, more than a hundred years old; the luxurious flowers in their ornamented vases, and by the galaxy of porcelain displayed behind glass.

Abbotsford was the first private residence ever to be lit by gas, generated by a plant in the grounds, and although the house is now illuminated by electricity the jets are still in their sockets, and the generator can still be seen in an outhouse.

Nor were we impressed by novelty, for we have already seen the splendours of the Palace of Holyroodhouse, the riches of Cullen House, Edinburgh Castle, Stirling Castle, not to mention Leith-Hall, Crathes Castle and Haddo House, but the literary environment of Abbotsford delighted me. Here I could live a recluse with the devotion of a monk. For the student of literature Abbotsford is a shrine, and the memory of its founder hallows it.

July 20th, Tuesday

Today I actually talked to a Countess, when we motored to Old Slains Castle, near Collieston, where I wanted to meet Mr. Martin Dickson, who published under the name of Michael Slains, but his landlady, the Countess of Hay and Erroll told me she thought he had gone abroad. She said nobody knew where Mr. Dickson had gone or if ever he would come back. I didn't tell the Countess why I wanted to see Mr. Dickson, but it really was to show him my short stories, with a view to printing an anthology, but now I'm afraid it shall have to wait.

The Countess lives in a chalet on a ledge of rock overlooking the sea, while Mr. Dickson's cottage is a bit further back from the edge of the cliff face. But such a frightful place to live in, and only a cart track to the old castle from the village of Collieston, itself famous for containing the burial place of one of our most notorious smugglers, namely Philip Kennedy, and where, in more recent times Lawrence of Arabia rented a cottage for his summer holidays over a number of years.

The old castle of Slains is a mere shell nowadays, and there is a danger of falling stones from its towering walls. It was destroyed personally by King James VI with gunpowder bought in Aberdeen, because the ninth Earl of Erroll was involved with the King of Spain in a plot to convert him to the Catholic faith and to dethrone Elizabeth of England. A Spanish galleon, the Santa Caterina, bringing stores and munitions to the Earl was wrecked in the bay under the castle, and the bay has ever since been known as St. Catherine's Dub, which would sound more appropriate as Tub.

Here in this tower lived Isabella of Buchan, the lady of courage who crowned the Bruce at Scone, and who was an ancestor of the present Countess, who has bought back the seat of her forefathers.

There were four donkeys on the grassy slopes, besides a goat and several ewes grazing among the cottages on the cliff top. Jane told me she used to play around these parts and she still remembered the "pinky braes" of her childhood flower picking, referring of course to the clusters of yellow primroses that grow profusely on the green slopes, persistently called "pinkies" despite their colour. Jane spent most of her school holidays with her aunt at a cottar house on the farm of Mains of Slains, which we passed on our way to the castle.

July 21st, Wednesday

We motored to Craigievar Castle, 26 miles from Aberdeen, similar to Crathes Castle on Deeside, which we visited last year. It comprises the old baronial style of Scottish building with graceful turrets and is said to be a perfect example of this type of castle. The usual carved ceilings and wood panelled walls; paintings, weapons, tapestries and books, but in this case very dark and gloomy in the small poky rooms because there is no electricity in the castle. Some of the paintings were by George Jamesone (1588-1644), Scotland's first portrait painter, who had a studio on Schoolhill brae in Aberdeen, where you can still see a commemoration tablet on the wall to mark the site.

The spiral staircase with a rope dangling for support when climbing to the higher rooms is exactly the same as at Crathes. Craigievar is the home of the Forbes Clan and this scion of the family still live there, though the building is under the care of the National Trust for Scotland. The motto over the doorway reads: Doe not Vaiken Sleiping Dogs.

The weather was misty and foul but the fir and birch trees beautiful even in their weeping state.

August 22nd, Sunday

We visited Glamis Castle, I with Jane and Grandma in the Austin A30 van. Glamis (pronounced Glams) is a magnificent baronial structure in beautiful surroundings and embodying many artistic and historical associations. It was the childhood home of the Queen of George VI (Queen Elizabeth Bowes Lyon, the Queen Mother), and their second daughter, Princess Margaret was born here. Glamis Castle is the supposed site of the murder of King Duncan by Macbeth, Thane of Glamis, and it is believed that Shakespeare visited the castle in 1590, where he conceived a setting for his only play based in Scotland. Yet three other sites, namely Duffus (near Nairn and the Witches' Heath of Forres), Inverness and Cawdor cry out to be blamed for the killing of the inglorious Duncan, to the utter confusion of the tourists and student novices of Scottish history. But King Malcolm II was certainly murdered here and the castle was garrisoned by Cromwell's troops during the Royalist Insurrection. Father and son, Charles I and James II face each other on pedestals at the entrance. Glamis is now the home of the Earl of Strathmore and his family.

The village of Glamis is secluded in trees on a bypass from the main Perth and Forfar road (A94), an operation which has been but recently completed. The Angus Folk Museum is housed in Kirk Wynd, a row of lovely old-world cottages behind the village, and is officiated by the National Trust for

Scotland. We were too late to gain admittance so we went to look at the church of St. Vigeans, originally older than Arbroath Abbey, and seemed like a picture out of a children's fairy-tale book, with its sagging roof and white slender spire against the dark green woods. I stopped the van and got out to try the massive wooden door in the Gothic portal, but it was locked. Across the road in the manse garden there is a ponderous lichened stone which is said to mark the grave of Malcolm II after his mortal wounds in the castle. The stone is sculptured with the fish and circle and other emblems which indicate its great age and Celtic origin. Baskets of fruit carved in stone and chalices of similar workmanship adorn the dykes surrounding the glebe, while I was greatly struck by the skull and cross-bones prominently etched on the stone gate-posts at the entrance to the old graveyard surrounding the kirk, which I usually associate with the scenery for J. M. Barrie's play THE LITTLE MINISTER.

The road disappeared under an archway, whither we proceeded with the van, to find ourselves back on the castle drive, where we made for the main road, and only just in time, for an old woman was about to close the gates.

August 28th, Saturday

By way of a change we motored to Braemar and the Linn o' Dee, where we saw several salmon leap over against the falls. Two people were accidentally drowned here on December 16th, 1927, and their names, Gwyn Gatensby and Katie Todd are etched on a stone overlooking the most dangerous part of the torrent, probably as a warning to others. The rocks are polished smooth and strangely pock marked by aeons of rushing water or by the movement of glaciers in the ice-age.

It was a beautiful day and the heather like a wine-red carpet on the hills and moors, and the green and yellow bracken thrown about in Nature's careless handfuls. I went into the lovely parish church in Braemar and read a little from the pulpit bible: "What man is he that desireth life, and loveth many days, that he may see good?" Ps. 34, 12. I read mostly wherever the minister has left his bible open, sometimes under a dust cover, and today's reading reflected my own thoughts of the morning, when I felt divinely pleased with life, and my mind seemed to glamorise everything my eyes lighted upon, forming pleasant conjecture and elevating my thoughts beyond reality. But this illusion of better things was rubbed off on the contacts of the day, like pollen from a butterfly's wings, but it was exhilarating while it lasted. It isn't often that this mood comes upon me, but when it does it is heavenly. I crave for knowledge with an imbiber's thirst, and to me poetry is the wine of life.

We were also at Crathie Church in the afternoon and just missed the Queen opening a sale of work in the local hall.

September 18th, Saturday

I went with Jane and Grandma in the van to see my father's gravestone in Old Deer cemetery. The stone has been newly cleaned and the lettering repainted at a cost of £3. 14s. 9d., which I recently paid from my mother's savings. The stone is situated at the far end of the cemetery, straight on from the main gate at the sexton's house, about the middle of the recent extension of the graveyard, on the left side of the path going in.

We went on to view the ruins of Strichen House, which, until now, has fascinated me from a distance. But I was determined to have a closer look, and so we motored up past the farm to see it, an old cart road of broom and whin that had once been the driveway to the mansion house, frequented by gilded ladies and their noblemen in horse carriages, now rutted with tractor wheels and churning with mud, while the mystery in stone before us revealed itself like a painter's dream. The present ruin was built in 1821 and was at one time occupied by the Frasers of Lovat. Dr. Samuel Johnson and James Boswell were here in 1788 (before the present residence was built) on their way to the Hebrides, having expressed a desire to see the remains of a Druidical temple on the estate. What remains of the mansion reveals an image of magnificent splendour, built in the Grecian style, with a portico of fluted Doric pillars, giving entrance over a basement to two storeys above ground. The remaining walls are still magnificent and impressive in their great height of beautifully dressed stonework, all quarried locally, and there are eight huge chimney-heads, rising nakedly only slightly higher than the walls, something in the style of the Adams' brothers, and indeed it would be surprising if they didn't have a share in its building. The structure is in a precarious state and could collapse in a thunder-clap. The policies are now a jungle of weeds where cattle and pigs meander at liberty and the huge walled garden is sown with corn. But seen from a distance, with the village and its spires in the foreground, Strichen House for me has all the wonder and romance of boyhood expectancy. It was at one time the home of Mary Garden, the Aberdeen soprano, where she employed a coachman to drive her about and she paid her servants with gold sovereigns.

We went afterwards through the village of Strichen, where my mother pointed out the house in Water Street where my father's people lived, though I have already forgotten it. An Englishman would probably pronounce the name as "Stricken", and looking at the white stone deer on Mormond Hill beyond the village he would probably come up with "Stricken Deer", though the villages of Old Deer and New Deer are several miles away. Situated in a romantic valley on the northern arm of the Ugie river it is one of Buchan's few beauty spots, an oasis almost in a harsh windswept landscape with scarcely more inundation than a stormy sea.

And so on to my own birthplace at Strathellie cottages, in the parish of Rathen, where the ancestors of Edvard Grieg, the Norwegian composer are buried, in the same graveyard as my own. I was born in the but-and-ben with its gable to the roadway and lived there till I was nearly eight years old. At that time the cottages were little better than hovels, with box-beds and thatched roofs, though they did have cement floors, but they have since been renovated and roofed with red slates.

From Strathellie cottages I first went to school at Lonmay. We went along with the van but I couldn't remember the way. Grandma directed us and I stopped the van at the school gates with a strange wonder in my mind. Here then, at this little out-of-the-way seminary I got my first instruction in learning; here I first stumbled through the alphabet and repeated the elementary tables of arithmetic, and here also I learned

my first recitation by heart, a snatch of which I still
remember:

> Up the airy mountain
> Down the rushy glen,
> We dare not go a haunting
> For fear of little men.

All of which has become such a treasure to me in later life.
I was a shy little boy, frightened and curious, and I could
hardly imagine now as I looked through the gates that I once
played and ate my "piece" in that little walled-in playground.
Here I found the golden key which later in life was to open my
mind to most of the greatest treasures in the English language,
though at the same time I was just beginning to master the
native doric of my fathers.

I went to Lonmay school when I was six in 1919 and
remained there for one year. From Lonmay I was transferred
to Blackhills school, when my parents moved to the farm of
Mains of Park in May, 1920. I remained here also for one year
"a cottar's lease", and then attended the Central School in
Peterhead until May 28th, 1923, when I was removed to
Coldwells school, near Longhaven in Cruden, until I was
twelve, when I was again transferred to Blackhills of Peterhead,
where I finished my schooling the day before I was fourteen,
on June 30th, 1927. I was considered a fair scholar, excelling
mostly in History, Geography and English, but my studies
were dissipated in truancy and idleness, except for the reading
of books.

Blackhills of Lonmay should not be confused with Blackhills
of Peterhead: I attended both these schools and both have now
been closed to teaching, the former now being used as a drying
kiln by local farmers for their grain.

October 15th, Friday

From a study of this itinerary to date one might get the
impression that my life was all play and no work, and thus of
little consequence in a commercialised community, but reading
the next entry on harvesting operations may help to dispel this
mistaken belief, though I will admit it has been one of the

easiest and certainly the shortest harvest season of nearly 40 years' experience on the land, due of course to the introduction of the combine-harvester on our farms. Indeed this is our first harvest undertaken completely by combine, the binders never having been yoked; and it is the first harvest in 28 years that I haven't built a corn stack. I started building in 1938 and every year since then I have built 40 to 50 stacks, sometimes more but very seldom less, as will be noted elsewhere in my journals. This then is our first harvest without the four 'S's, namely, scythes, sheaves, stooks and stacks. So there.

1966

On Tuesday evening, February 15th, I drove to Cadger's Garage at Belhelvie to have our van tested—steering, brakes and lighting for another year of reasonably safe motoring. The test is now compulsory and cost me 15/-, of which one shilling goes to the Government, and the certificate with which I was furnished will keep me on the right side of the law for another year of Travels Without a Donkey. This is the third year running that our Austin A30 van has passed the roadworthy test without need of repair or expense, and I think this repays my careful handling and servicing of our vehicle.

May 15th, Sunday

Our first run of the year took us to St. Mary's Parish Church at Monymusk, which is twelfth-century Norman design and one of the oldest churches in Scotland still used for public worship, second only perhaps to the Church of St. Michael at Linlithgow. Monymusk in the Gaelic is from Monadh-muice, "the Boar's Hill", but speaking figuratively it implies "the land of many deer", and judging by the surrounding hills and magnificent woodlands such an appellation would be justified. In the church there is a very old bible purchased for the diocese in the reign of Charles II. It is fitted with clasps and had probably once been chained but now lies open under glass, so that I couldn't lay hands on it, which was maybe just as well, because in those days the letter "s" was printed like an "f", and this gives me terrible bother once I get started.

There used to be a Priory here but all that remains of it are parts of the Tower and church walls. The first missionaries were the Culdees, those "Servants of God" who were probably the followers of St. Finan from Whithorn who came north to establish a mission among the heathen, improvising with wattle huts and stone and mud cells and church before they built the Priory, at the behest of Queen Margaret and Malcolm Canmore, who had rested from battle here after one of his forays to subdue the rebels of Moray. The building was

completed early in the first half of the twelfth century, even
before the establishment of the Bishopric of Aberdeen, and was
subject to the mother church of the Augustinian Order in
Scotland, St. Andrew's Cathedral in Fife. For nearly four
centuries the Priory flourished at Monymusk, but with the
national outcry against Papal authority it fell into disrepute
and was eventually destroyed by fire.

John Wesley twice preached in the present church of
Monymusk during his Scottish tours. His daily walks in the
parish inspired him to write in his journal of the beauty of the
landscape, the glory of the trees and on the excellent singing
of the congregation.

But there are traces of human habitation in Monymusk long
before the Christian Saints crossed the mountains to convert
the inhabitants to the New Faith. Beakers and Pictish symbol
stones have been unearthed by the plough over the centuries,
and there are traces of man from the Stone, Bronze and Iron
Ages, when the Caterthuns or hill forts of the neighbourhood
were still occupied and defended, perhaps a thousand years
before the Crucifixion.

But like the Shroud of Turin a relic of the Christian Faith
has survived at Monymusk. It is the Brecbannoch, more
commonly known as The Monymusk Reliquary, dating from
the seventh-century A.D., now in the National Museum of
Antiquities, Queen Street, Edinburgh. This is the most
priceless surviving relic of the Celtic Church in Scotland, and
it originally contained a bone of St. Columba of Iona. This
bone of the Saint was carried before the Scots army at Bannockburn, like the Ark of the Covenant was carried by the Children
of Israel in the Promised Land. Until 1933 the Reliquary was
kept in the House of Monymusk, home of the Grant family,
hereditary lairds of Monymusk, and when John Barbour wrote
his immortal poem on THE BRUCE he lived only nine miles
away at Old Rayne, where he was a minister and schoolmaster,
and must have known of its existence, moreso when he became
Archdeacon of Aberdeen in 1357. Barbour was well qualified
to write the history of THE BRUCE, and although he penned it
some sixty years after the death of his hero some eye-witness
accounts were still available to him. He was also well placed
geographically, living within sight of the hill which gave its

name to the Battle of Barra, between Inverurie and Old-meldrum, where the outworks of a pre-historic fort are still plainly visible from the main roads in the area.

Leaving Monymusk we motored through the Lord's Throat and Paradise Valley on the banks of the river Don, a beautiful vista of lime-green birch trees and sparkling waters, reminiscent of the Trossachs in central Scotland. On the road above Tullynessle, from the summit of the Suie Hill (1,362 ft) one obtains one of the finest viewpoints in Aberdeenshire, with Knockespock Castle in the wooded valley; the hill of Tap o' Noth in the middle distance at Rhynie, and the countryside of farming land and heathered hill mapped out in a panoramic curve to Culsalmond.

Rhynie is one of my favourite villages and here I made a most remarkable discovery. In the village are some very old houses, homes of the people of a former century, characteristic of their age and period, and on the front wall of one of these houses, facing the square, is a metal plaque commemorating the birth of MACKAY OF UGANDA, October 13th, 1849, and also his death at Usambiro, Uganda, Central Africa, on February 8th, 1890. It is indeed remarkable how many of our tiny Scots villages have given a valorous son to history and immortality. Here in Rhynie, a son of the Free Kirk Manse became one of the most distinguished missionaries ever to enter the then Dark Continent of Africa, where he established such a faith in the natives for his doctrine that they long remembered him as Mackay Lubare dala! "Mackay is the Great Spirit!" Mackay was a selfless, dedicated servant of Christianity whose super-human efforts in easing the distress of the suffering African tribes is faithfully recorded in the Church Missionary archives in London. So we have our Mungo Parks and our David Livingstones in the quite timeless hearthstones of rural Aberdeenshire, where the people go about their daily business without the slightest knowledge of it.

Mackay's father, the Reverend Dr. Alexander Mackay, was the first Free Kirk minister in Rhynie, a worthy character from the brimming pages of JOHNNY GIBB OF GUSHETNEUK, which was sited at Chapel of Garioch, if not partly written there, about eight miles horse-ride east of Rhynie. The Mackays were resident in Rhynie until 1867, when the family moved to

Edinburgh, and as the first edition of JOHNNY GIBB appeared
only four years later, in 1871, it is quite feasible to suppose
that the author, William Alexander, had some acquaintance
with this very first Free Kirk minister of Rhynie, and that he
drew upon his character for one of his incumbents in the famous
classic, which had the innovation of the Free Kirk Presbytery
as its principal theme.

Another literary coincidence is that Mackay of Uganda
attended the Grammar School in Aberdeen where Lord Byron
had been an earlier pupil. Perhaps it is to the credit of the
masters of the Grammar School, as much as to the ability of
their scholars, that they produced Byron as a great poet and
Mackay as a bible translator, when in later years he transcribed
several books of the bible into the Luganda language for his
African converts. The explorer Henry Stanley described
Mackay as "the best missionary I ever knew", and he had
known the great Dr. David Livingstone.

Later we came by Alford, which is Charles Murray country,
with the cottage of his birth by the roadside (1864-1941), and a
plaque on the wall. Here we have another Scot who spent his
life in Africa, in the sunnier sphere of the South Cape, where
he became so very homesick that he wrote all those wonderful
doric poems that are still enjoyed by Scots everywhere.

Here we had tea by the roadside and Jane filled the back of
the van with kindling sticks from the wood. Actually we had
stopped where the old Alford, Kemnay-Kintore railway runs
parallel with the road, but of course the rails and sleepers have
gone and only the embankments remain for future historians
to trace its course.

Oldmeldrum is another Aberdeenshire village which can
boast of a prodigal son, "a lad o' pairts", from a humble and
obscure background who became world famous as "The
Father of Tropical medicine". On the South Road from the
village, at the house on Cromlet Hill, there is a plaque set in a
stone tablet commemorating the birth of Sir Patrick Manson
(1845-1922), who pioneered the theory that malaria was
carried by the mosquito from the disease infested swamps to
humans in the orient, and thus enabled scientific research to
cope with this fatal and dreaded tropical malady. Manson
graduated from Aberdeen University and for many years

practised in Amoy and Hong-Kong, where he studied tropical diseases and medicinal cures while caring for his patients. He was knighted in 1903.

Mary Slessor, the renowned African missionary was born in Aberdeen but her mother came from Oldmeldrum, where in Urquhart Road a block of houses is still known as Mary Slessor Place. She was in Calibar, West Africa, throughout the period that Mackay from Rhynie was in Uganda. They both arrived in Africa the same year, 1876, but while Mackay perished in 1890 Mary Slessor survived in Calibar until her death in 1915. Wouldn't it be interesting to try and find out if they were acquainted, or even if each knew of the other's existence. Probably not, for the world was a much bigger place then, with little means of communication.

June 6th, Monday

Today we went for a whistle stop tour of some of the villages on the Moray Firth coast. Starting with Portsoy we moved west to Cullen, Portknockie, Findochty, Portessie and Buckie, omitting Portgordon because it was getting late, and motored home via Keith, Huntly and Inverurie. Of all these villages (and towns), primarily situated as fishing ports, but now almost defunct for that purpose, I think that from an artist's viewpoint Cullen is the most beautiful. Viewed from the top of the High Street, with the sea framed in the arch at the bottom, and the church steeple on the right, Cullen provides a colourful and romantic vista. And once through the arch we have the majestic railway viaduct which to me is only equalled by the viaduct at Berwick-on-Tweed and the one at Glenfinnan, at the head of Loch Sheil, near Prince Charlie's monument. If I had seen bridges like these as a boy I may have become an engineer like Telford or General Wade, but I had to be content with much smaller bridges, and less inspiring ones, across the Ugie.

Weird rock formations are also a feature of the seascape at Cullen, chief of which are the Three Kings on the shorefront, backed by stacks of red sandstone and green sloping cliffs sprinkled with yellow primroses, and the sea a heaving blue-green transparency, breaking into froth around the rocks while the gulls breast and dip in the waves like tiny Viking ships, the younger of them apparently unable to rise directly from the water.

We were also intrigued by the fishermen's houses on the waterfront, each one gaily painted in various colours, from stone blue to cherry pink, each one trying to outshine his neighbour in a colour pattern. But not only the doors and windows are painted, indeed the woodwork seems to be of secondary consideration, and is sometimes varnished to give a shine; but the houses are painted stone by stone, jamb and lintel, and even the pointing outlined, and the effect seems to characterise the house-proud, tight-fisted, God-fearing, courageous fishermen who no longer work here, but labour elsewhere for a living, or live by the tourists on bed and breakfast rivalry.

House painting seems to be a mania among the fisher folk on the Moray Coast, although it is less noticeable in the Buchan towns. All these villages are the same, from Sandhaven and Pitullie in the east to Hopeman and Burghead in the west, but I think that the laurel must go to Lossiemouth for sheer artistic beauty. It was here in the birthplace of Ramsay Macdonald that I first noticed the painted houses of the fishermen: each window a showpiece of respectability and domestic bliss, curtained with expensive, shimmering material, and in the centre invariably a huge lusciously green Lily of the Nile in a brass or porcelain pot on a fretted hallstand table of varnished wood. The personality of the fisherman's wife is in her front windows facing the street, and if you want a glimpse of her husband's character go down and look at the painted boats in the Lossiemouth harbour, where the net-balls are as gay and varied as the balloons at a festival. Such an advertisement of self-expression and sheer devotion to life, and but for the absence of garden flowers would make a paradise of this withering coastline.

June 11th, Saturday

Runabout tour with Jane and Grandma in the van, via— Logierieve, Esslemont, Ellon, Arnage, Stuartfield, Mintlaw, Longside, Rora, Crimond, Rattray (the lighthouse), Rathen, Cairness, Lonmay, Kilbirnie (Grandma's childhood home), Strichen, Old Deer, Arnage, Ellon, Foveran and home. We left home about 2 p.m. and arrived back at 10 o'clock. We stopped at the very old chapel at Rattray (not to be confused with the village of Rattray at Blairgowrie) roofless and ivy covered and some quaint old gravestones in the graveyard. Grandma stayed in the van while Jane and I walked down to the water's edge to look at Rattray Head lighthouse through our binoculars. You can walk right out to it over the rocks when the tide is out but today the water was lapping the seaweed on the shore. It was a beautiful day but the horizon was blue and hazy. The fields and roads here are hedged with hawthorn, at this season a very froth of white blossom, and the warm air scented with the sweet nostalgic smell of it, like a perfume fresh from heaven's pharmacy, lodging in the rain drops in the small white flower cups. I am usually transported by the sickening sweet smell of it and I pulled some nosegays and stuck them up in the van, though Jane won't have them in the house, because it is unlucky she says to give them house room. I also cut a bunch of lusciously red rhododendrons from the wasted grounds at Cairness House, a magnificent mansion now unoccupied, except for some chickens in the old servants' quarters at the back. Viewed from a distance, nestling among the trees of Cairness Woods, I have always compared this beautiful structure with Nottingham Castle on the backs of Player's cigarette packets; but undoubtedly it is after a design of the Adams brothers or their famous father, and since the last laird died it was latterly used as a guest house.

Back on the main road I stopped the van for a peep through the broken windows of St. Columba's Chapel at Lonmay, where the vandals have made a shambles of this beautiful sanctuary. What was held sacred by an older generation now seems worthless and without meaning, and I just wonder what our ancestors who worshipped here would think of their wonderful chapel if they could see it now, one of my own forefathers among them, on my mother's side, who was a verger here for many years and now asleep in the churchyard. The pews have been removed and the floor is a litter of broken glass, the plaster crumbling from the sacred walls and the altar desecrated. Perhaps one of the local farmers will make use of the chapel as a garage for combine-harvesters, with a big door punched in the gable to get the good of the high vaulted roof to let the monsters inside, which is what has been happening with a great many of our country churches in recent years, a sign of the times.

On Sunday, June 12th, we took the A974 from Aberdeen to Tarland and stopped one mile beyond Echt to look at the magnificent Sunhoney Stone Circle, one of the most complete Druidical arenas in the British Isles. Not a stone is missing and the site is well protected by a stone dyke and fence. The circle is within a small copse of trees which can be seen from the road, just behind Sunhoney Farm. And such a delightful name, like that other farm near Kildrummy in Strathdon—Honeybarrel; and there's Honeyneuk of Maud, down in Buchan, all of which reminds me of the townman who said to his bed and breakfast landlady: "This is capital honey; may I ask, do you keep a bee?" There are nine upright stones at Sunhoney, and two flankers, one on each side of the altar stone, which is rich in cupmark symbols and measures 17 feet across and probably weighs 10 to 15 tons, or even more. The vertical stones are roughly 30 feet apart, forming a wide grass-grown clearance. The altar or flanker stones are nearly eight feet above ground and have probably stood there since 1500 B.C. We next visited the ruined fane of St. Nidan in the hollow by the stream at the foot of the Hill of Fare, close by the A974 from Aberdeen to Tarland. Here I met a man named Robert Tocher who, like myself, is extremely interested in these historic sites and we had a lively blether together on such matters. But unlike Jane his wife sat in the car and shared none of his enthusiasm.

And thus to New Kirk, Mid Mar, where the Church of Christ and a Pagan Circle of the Druids stand cheek by jowl in the kirkyard. I suppose that nowhere else in Britain could you see this juxtaposition of religious contrast in such close proximity. Three of the monoliths are missing but the altar stones are of enormous dimension, and the flat stone 15 feet long and nearly shoulder high from the ground. In the words of Cuthbert Graham, our local press authority on such matters of antiquity: "Its enormous monoliths rise up from the edge of a neatly shaven lawn with a shout of Pagan exuberance". I went into the rather gloomy church, cap in hand, almost tip-toe, to sniff the gorgeous white lilies on a table in front of the pulpit. I felt like an intruder on sacred ground, but I stayed long enough to read some of the plaques for the dead of the parish on the walls, while the larch trees, like shrouded saints in green, whispered at the windows.

We went on to Tarland, where we stopped in the Square for ice-cream and I put three gallons of petrol in the van. And thus back to Aboyne and home by the North Deeside road. There was a lack of sun which gave the colours a soft deep appearance and made the trees seem richly green. Laburnum was hanging in rich yellow tassels by the roadside and the broom was like feathered gold on the misty hills. Mountain Ash now white with blossom and scenting the air with its fragrance. A lot of cars on the roads but we arrived home about 9.30 in the evening without mishap.

June 26th, Sunday

We went to Pitcaple Castle, near Inverurie, in Aberdeenshire. A soft rain was falling on the trees and grass and we were glad to get inside when we left the van. The Laird was in his kilt and waiting for us at the top of the stone steps by the huge studded door. He is over six feet, a stalwart man who suited his kilt well, as it does most of these Highland chieftains, standing nearly head and shoulders above average height. Captain Burgess Lumsden by name he accepted our two half-crowns and gave us a short history of the castle while we waited for other sightseers to arrive. It is a private residence still lived in but excepting the bedrooms we were shown every nook and peephole in the castle, from kitchen basement to the highest pinnacles of the round pointed towers, banqueting hall, the Laird's Lug (where he listened to the gossip of the servants), the secret passage where the great Marquis of Montrose was offered an escape route but refused it, everything.

King James IV of Scotland visited here in the days before Flodden, about the same time as he used the Hunting Lodge at Caskieben, nearer Aberdeen, and went deer stalking on the Tyrebagger Hill. After a strenuous day on the hill the king declared: "She's a tiring bugger, bring the caskie ben", and thus these places were named, and likewise Dyce, nearby, from his having a throw at the game to pass the time on misty days, when it was too wet to go on the Tyrebagger, and you could add with appropriate euphony that in modern times many a tyre has been buggered on that same brae.

Charles II was also at Pitcaple before the days of Cromwell and his Roundheads, and we were shown the room the monarch slept in, the King's Room, with an entrancing view of the mountain of Bennachie from the window, like the heel of a giant's shoe discarded on the summit. Mary Queen of Scots danced on the green in front of the house, where a tree marks the area traversed by her dainty feet. The Marquis of Montrose was led here captive from the battle of Carbisdale, on the Kyle of Sutherland, in 1650, on his way to execution in Edinburgh. On the eve of his departure the Lady of the castle crept to his dungeon to show him the secret passage of escape, but rather than undergo such a claustrophobic experience he chose to face the hangman.

The library contains a complete set of the Waverley Novels, all of Dickens and Thackeray; some delightful paintings, family portraits, etchings, silverware and richly carved furniture.

At Pitcaple castle I saw a fiddle-sower for the first time in my life, much as I have heard of them in my 40 years on the land. This instrument is carried in front of the sower and requires the action of a fiddle-bow to distribute the corn on the furrows.

I went into the parish kirk at Keig while it was still raining. The usual musty smell that empty kirks have, a stale sniff of departed humanity, and the sacred silence, with nobody there but God in his empty house. Plaques on the walls all devoted to deceased ministers of the parish. Electric light and heating, the walls in a dull salmon pink and the woodwork in lilac grey. The view from the churchyard in Todd—AO and colour De Luxe, to use a cinematic expression; the colours deep and soothing, beautifully soft; the patches of young bracken mapped in pale green on the brown panorama of encircling hills, the trees huddled in rich clusters in the valley of the Don. And all the while the rain played a soft sweet symphony on the sun-glanced leaves, like a whispering to the dead in their lonely tombs. Churches are my focal points of observation on a parish; here I take my bearings and identify myself with my surroundings. And so on to Alford, where Balfluig Castle is just across the fields, and home by Monymusk, Kemnay and Fintray.

33

July 3rd, Sunday

I motored with Jane to Drum Castle, just beyond the village of Culter (pronounced Cooter) on lovely Deeside, holiday valley of the Kings and Queens of Britain from the days of Victoria and Albert. Rich beautiful furnishings in the newer part of the house, dated 1619 and still lived in by the Irvine family, from the days of Robert the Bruce, who used the seat as a hunting lodge. One of the Irvines was his armour-bearer and as a reward he was granted the lands of Drum by the king. Two of the fireplaces are particularly beautiful, one richly carved in wood, probably teak, as a wedding present to a former bride of Drum. Two of the ceilings are magnificent, panelled in oak without a nail in it, and treated every two years with a preservative oil which brings out a richer colour than any paint or varnish could imitate. The library is in the old keep, above the dungeon and below the guardroom, and likewise with a barrel roof and a casement window let into a wall which is nine feet thick. Walls of the keep lined with priceless books and a cloth covered chair in a corner, a chair it is said which was used to house the doup of Mary Queen of Scots when she visited the castle, about the time she watched the battle of Corrichie, from the Hill of Fair, not far distant, when she sat on a hard stone and watched brave men butcher each other for her favours—surely the epitome of vanity in womanhood. Another Queen Mary, but a far more gracious and humane lady, wife of George V was twice at Drum, and her charming photo stands on the mantelshelf in the library.

We climbed the old keep to the battlements, where the view is inspiring and romantic, even for a queen, and the tall fir trees standing like plumed sentinels in the lush green surroundings; each glance through the magic turrets more exciting than the former, and even the roofs and chimneys like a fairyland from this altitude. The square tower dates from the twelfth century and is well preserved; one of the very best in all Scotland, and must have looked much the same to a jubilant Bruce resting after Bannockburn.

Of all the Scottish castles we have visited Drum is unique in being intact as an original structure. Indeed I never before have

seen such a fine example of the tower keep, unless it be compared with the bell tower at Dunkeld Cathedral. Unlike
Pitcaple Castle, which I tried to describe last Sunday, there
was a conspicuous absence of antlered stag heads and hunting
trophies, period uniforms and weaponry, and prehistoric
pottery; but Drum is rich in chinaware, pictures and carpets,
and an abundance of period French clocks, ornamented with
brass on marble. The keep was renovated in 1961.

Drum is also famous for its ballad about the laird who went
a hunting and fell in love with a "well faured" (beautiful)
maid a shearing her father's barley, probably one of the
crofters on his estate.

> "My bonnie may, my weel-faur'd may,
> O will you fancy me, O;
> And gae and be the Lady o' Drum,
> And lat your shearing a-be, O?"

> "My father he is a shepherd mean,
> Keeps sheep on yonder hill, O,
> And ye may gae and speer at him,
> For I am at his will, O."

> Peggy Coutts is a very bonnie bride,
> And Drum is a wealthy laddie,
> But he might hae chosen a higher match,
> Than ony shepherd's lassie.

But of course they were wed and lived happily ever after,
and in the last of twenty-four verses the laird declares his
humility and life-long devotion to the crofter's daughter:

> "For an' I war dead, and ye war dead,
> And baith in ae grave laid, O,
> And ye and I war tane up again,
> Wha could tell yer mools frae mine, O?"

This has been our best view yet of a Scottish baronial
mansion in its original state, except perhaps for Crathes and
Craigievar, where there are some features of distinction in this
respect. Admission was half-a-crown each and worth it.

July 6th, Wednesday

Three more hours on serious overtime. But I am as tough as nails or I could never stand the strain of it with the younger men. I seem to toughen with the years and I am little the worse at the end of a day. My hands are like vice-grips from long grasping of the hoe-handle. Men with soft hands blister easily. I am resilient and easily rested. A short nap and a bite to eat and I am fighting fit again. I am a slow starter but I can stay on the job once I get going and I don't easily let go of the stick. All my life I have been too much accustomed to long hard struggling battles to be easily beaten now. Life has inured me to siege and to patient endurance in adversity. But ah ha! Holidays are just around the corner again: two weeks when I can enjoy a social freedom and forget the timetable of existence; two weeks when I can be my own boss and do what I like and go anywhere I please—within reason, and I have assured myself that I shall enjoy it. I shall go on holiday without a qualm of conscience, satisfied that I have done my bit for God's world and that I justly deserve a break, because I have never been on strike in my life and I have never been in a dole queue, and the only holidays I ever enjoyed in my youth were in convalescence after an illness. No, I am not conceited; merely thankful that my lot has improved. And if you say that I have the unions to thank for that I will reply that you are wrong, because our membership is too weak to assert itself, and that our emancipation is owing to the fact that so many younger men are leaving the land and making it more attractive for those who stay, their services more appreciated.

But enough of politics, for on Sunday, July 17th, as a prelude to the holidays, we went for a run to Strathdon, that beautiful vale of pale green birch and rolling sun-kissed hills, with skies that smile and weep by turns, like the eyes of a maid in love. We left the car on a grassy slope on a crook of the Don and walked up the old cart road to the ruins of Glenbuchat Castle, a weary sentinel of the years on the eastern flank of Ben Newe, that heavenly mountain, like a resting lion stroked by the hand of God.

This Scottish Tower House was built by a John Gordon and his wife Helen Carnegie in 1590 and sold to Lord Brace' (later

Earl of Fife) in 1738 by a later John Gordon, a prominent Jacobite. The Gordons of Glenbuchat were a race of Highlanders greatly feared by their enemies, an apprehension that extended even to Royalty and the House of Hanover, and George II had such a horror at the name of this chieftain that he often dreamed of him, starting in his sleep, crying out in broken English: "De great Glenbucket be coming!" But of course he had reason to fear revenge for his brother's treatment of the Highlanders after the '45 rebellion, and maybe his conscience was more tender than that of Butcher Cumberland.

The last Gordon of Glenbuchat was a devout Jacobite and escaped to France after Culloden in 1746, where he died in ripe old age. Yet it is said of him that he was a man of letters and great accomplishment, and his motto reads: NOTHING ON EARTH REMAINS BOT FAME, which seems to justify his lust for living so defiantly in such dangerous times. The castle was destroyed by fire in a former absence, burnt by his enemies while he was out in a foray against one of the neighbouring clans. Helen Carnegie's name is still above the door, carved in stone, much the same as Henrietta Gordon at Huntly Castle, but less prominent. And it is such a pity one reflects that the Stuarts were so devoutly averse to changing their religion, for if they had renounced Catholicism to become Protestants there would never have been a House of Hanover in England and the whole course of world history would have been stabilised, perhaps even to averting the 1914 war with Germany.

We walked back to the car and motored round the shoulder of Ben Newe, crossing the water of Buchat on a narrow stone bridge towards the little church on the crest of the mountain, where I am told it is half-a-mile to the princely summit. And such an entrancing view from this lonely old chapel of Glenbuchat, with the history of the parish in its walled in graveyard, where death seems but a hush of silent ecstasy, the sun lighting up the valley and the corries in the hills in pastel hues, soft and hazy and so diverting in their barren glory. In the centre of the valley is the old Free Church and a pottery, surrounded by the farmsteads that crouch on the hillsides. Once over the Buchat again I stopped the car and Jane got out to pull some

"Wild Mountain Thyme" by the roadside, and a bunch of silver grass for her vases on the sideboard. The road through Glenbuchat circles inland among the hills and emerges at Strathdon village where the Water of Nochty joins the river Don.

July 21st, Thursday

It was yesterday that we set out for a week's touring in the south of Scotland and northern England, where I plan to walk on Hadrian's wall and stand on the battlefield of Flodden (1513). We slept the first night in the van near Louden Hill, where Bruce defeated the Earl of Pembroke in 1306, his first real success against the English. We were on the site of a derelict railway station, near a crumbling old viaduct of 13 arches, each one like a picture frame with the most gorgeous scenery behind it, green rolling hills mantled with trees and white farmsteads in the sleepy valleys, like the water-colours teacher used to hang on the classroom walls for art study, or the marvellous calendars we sometimes get at Hogmanay—only this was the real thing, and the effect on the beholder was entrancing. The viaduct is splendid even in decay, spanning the valley on its massive pillars, a lesson on social history, and the roadway, the cause of its disuse, running beneath one of its arches. The bridge is in a dangerous condition and may have to be demolished, lest its parapets topple on the cattle and sheep pasturing in the valley. I walked some way across the viaduct, on the old cinder track, where the sleepers had been on the line to Darvel, and I suppose that Sir Harry Lauder had travelled by this branch railway many times on his wanderings from Strathnaven. And such a thrill it was to survey the countryside from this vantage point, and to ruminate on its building, its history and its decay; but that fear seized me over the third or fourth arch, where the viaduct seemed to get taller and the other end of it more remote and narrow, so that I couldn't have crossed it even for a wager, at least not alone, and as I stood by the windy parapet it seemed like part of a nightmare dream, where you always wake up just before the plunge. The terrifying spectacle from some of these viaducts has somewhat sobered the desire of my youth to become an

38

engine driver on the railways, where the prospect from the footplate would have been more exacting, more nerve-wracking than from the cosy corner of a carriage window.

We slept in the van by the old railway yard, and had scarcely bedded down when a vanload of noisy youths drove up quite near us to spend the night, drinking and jeering long after dark. There were girls' voices among them, with a Glasgow accent, and we feared that they were hooligans and became anxious for our safety, but at last we fell asleep in the midst of their hilarity.

This morning when we awoke all was quiet, though the big white van with our intruders was still in the railway yard, the occupants sound asleep, but they had not molested us. We were almost eaten alive by midges over breakfast and we finished up as quickly as possible, glad to get on the road to Darvel, where we stopped at the public conveniences. Here it was warm with a gorgeous sun and a slight soft breeze that dispelled the midges. I am writing this in the van at Darvel, beside an old lodge with honeysuckle at the gates and masons' trestles at the door and the public park just over the bridge behind us.

We spent a most wonderful day in Ayr: absolutely delightful and the hot sun filming everything in paint pot colours. We visited the Tam o' Shanter Inn but skipped Burns' cottage and the Auld Brig o' Doon because we saw these on an earlier visit four years ago. I took a photograph of the magnificent spire on the Louden Hall and snapped the Auld Brig o' Ayr on my knee, through the parapet of the newer bridge, though here my joy was marred by the presence of a drunk lying in his vomit. We posted six postcards home and Jane bought some small gifts for the family.

I have turned another page and I am writing this in a layby near Butlin's Holiday Camp and the Heads of Ayr, where I photographed a vintage locomotive on show by the roadside. It is now 6.50 and the sun still blazing down on us like a scorching searchlight. I got a can of water from the farmer at Pennyglen, ten miles south of Ayr, and we had a lively discussion on the economics of agriculture, and of the adamant "couldn't care less" attitude of the Government and the people concerning our stifled efforts to feed them. We spent the night in a big public layby near Culzean Castle, where two men, one with a beard, stopped their car and set up a tent just behind us.

July 22nd, Friday

I got up about seven and washed and shaved in the morning sun. We breakfasted on spartan fare and fed the birds. The two men have taken down their tent and are both seated on a white pillar by the roadside. It is now 9 a.m. and we are waiting until Culzean Castle opens at ten o'clock. We spent four hours in the castle and grounds, including the spacious walled gardens, and we went for a pleasant walk in Happy Valley, around Swan Lake and along the cliff-tops back to the castle. Tropical weather and date palms in the castle grounds and a graceful fountain spraying the lawns with a fine mist. Beautiful Adam ceilings in the castle and the famous oval staircase, pillared on three flights of Doric, Corinthian and Roman porticos. Queen Anne, Chippendale, Jacobean and Georgian furnishings, a host of beautifully rich paintings, weapons and armoury of all sorts and the most decorative and most voluble music box I have ever heard playing.

The castle was designed and built by Robert Adam around 1786 for the Kennedy family, who have been Earls of Cassillis for nearly 500 years. Could this be a scion of the late President Kennedy's family, who had their roots in Ireland?—and probably why ex-President Eisenhower enjoys a suite of rooms in the castle during his golfing tours for his leadership of the Allies to victory in the last war.

We looked at Ailsa Craig, "Paddy's Milestone", through our glasses from the coast road, comparing its size with a steamer passing the rock at the time. We stopped for a few minutes in Girvan, and at Ballantrae (not forgetting Stevenson's novel) and then on to dinner in a draughty quarry on the road to Stranraer. For dinner we had meat soup, rice crispies, ice-cream and prunes, most of it from tins or cartons, and our milk also, which I got from a slot machine at Girvan, all of which is a credit to the ingenuity of our manufacturers in the scientific preparation of food for the tourist, and also as it is a great boost to trade and employment and commerce in general.

All we had to do was light up our little stove with methylated spirit and heat the stuff, and hey presto—it's ready!

Three gallons of Shell petrol at Glenluce at 5/3d. a gallon and fifteen minutes in Newton Stewart. Tea at the head of Wigtown Bay. Time now 8 o'clock. Sky dull and overcast and mist on the hills. Looked at Carsluith Castle on the shores of Wigtown Bay, and also at Cardoness Castle, overlooking the Water of Fleet, both ancient monuments in the care of the Ministry of Works. We slept in an eerie layby south of Dalbeattie. Jane thought she heard footsteps behind the hedge after dark. We imagined all sorts of terrible things happening to us and couldn't go to sleep. I wasn't really scared but concerned for our safety and I blamed Jane for refusing to go into a camping site. She is somewhat shy of strangers and likes privacy and because of this we have slept in all sorts of queer places up and down the country. But this sort of disturbance is bringing her round to my way of thinking and I believe that next year we will go into a site. I was ever so thankful when another car came in and lit up the layby with its headlights, and when they switched them off we felt sure they would be staying the night. But I was still on the defensive and fell asleep around midnight with a bottle in my hand. If anyone should enter the van I was determined to have the first crack at him; moreso because the van door on my side doesn't lock.

July 23rd, Saturday

It is now the morning and we have realised such fools we were in the dark, because the footsteps we thought we heard behind the hedge was merely a bunch of friendly cows plucking grass. We laughed at our fears in broad daylight but it wasn't such fun in the dark, in a strange place and so far from home we had all sorts of sinister forebodings. But now the sun was up and the mist was rising and we began to take in the beauty of our surroundings in big deep breaths of thankfulness. It was a new day again and everything was lovely in the sun-glint, so we breakfasted in the van and made off as soon as we could, while the car behind us was still blinded with newspapers in the windows.

We stopped in Dalbeattie to buy provisions and to telephone

Graham in Aberdeen, just to make sure everything was all
right at home. Well you never know, somebody could die and
we wouldn't know about it, so I made sure, though it cost me
4/3d. for peace of mind. Dalbeattie is a quiet little place so
early in the morning and no parking problems: no yellow
lines on the streets and no traffic wardens; I just swung into
the kerb and stopped wherever there was an empty space.
After phoning, and while Jane went shopping I walked over to
the local Picture House to have a look at their stills and show
bills. This is something I like to do in most of the small towns
we pass through. It's like meeting old friends in far-away places,
or someone we have known at home, and even the familiarity
of television has not robbed, or "cured" me of this nostalgia—
rather increased it with all these old movies we have been
seeing lately. At Dalbeattie they were showing Walt Disney's
"That Darned Cat", quite a new film for a small town hall,
but they had Bingo two nights a week, and this is what is
happening in most country towns where they can scarcely
support a cinema—thanks to television.

We had tea and wrote postcards at Sweetheart Abbey, a
beautiful ruin in red sandstone with a tradition that goes deep
in Scottish history, and with the founding of Balliol College,
Oxford. My little guide leaflet speaks about "The ruined,
rose-coloured walls of Sweetheart Abbey—one of the three
Cistercian abbeys of Galloway, look out across Solway Firth
to the Cumberland hills beyond. Much of the work dates from
the early fourteenth century, a period of unrest in Scotland
that saw little building; the ruins are, for this reason, of special
interest".

The traffic at Dumfries was like a race of spinning-tops and I
had to queue at the traffic lights. The answer to finding your
way out of a strange town of any size is by checking your road
numbers on a map and watching for them carefully on the
road signs. I have learned from frustrating experience that
the name of the place you are looking for is less important
than the number of the road: several names may be on the
boards by the time you get there, and always one ahead of the
one you seek, but the number is always right and won't lead
you astray if you follow it carefully. Before we left on this
present trip I spent a whole evening mapping the routes we

should take, noting the number of every road we should travel, and the name of every town we would be passing through; so we are not here by accident, but by careful reckoning, almost to the hour, as if it were a royal entourage. Jane has nothing to do with this but she gives me credit always for a well planned itinerary. Oh yes, I make mistakes to be sure, and sometimes lose my temper in the busy towns, but all things considered, and the weather giving me a chance I am anything if not methodical where our holidays are concerned.

And why? you may ask, should I be in such a hurry to get out of so lovely a place as Dumfries? Didn't I know that this was where Bruce killed the Red Comyn? That a plaque on a wall marks the site of the church where it happened? Didn't I know that Burns died here, in the narrow cobbled street named after him, formerly Mill Street, with the two-storey house at the end? That we could visit St. Michael's Church where Burns worshipped, the very pew he sat in, and his mausoleum in marble? And I will answer that I know all these things (or how else could I write them down) and that we have already seen all these places on a former visit, so we mustn't waste time here. Even before we left home I knew we would spend about ten minutes in Dumfries, allowing for traffic jams, so now we are on our way again. Besides I am hungry, and we must find a place where we can park and light the stove for dinner.

We found such a place on the Nith estuary, on the Caerlaverock Nature Conservancy, where there are warning signs to bathers about quicksands and swift tides all along the road. I swept the mud flats with my glasses and I could pick out numerous wildfowl on the river. For dinner we had chicken broth, fresh strawberries and ice-cream (bought at Dalbeattie) tea and rice biscuits. Gee! but this is better than work, a thousand times better if you know how to enjoy life on a modest income. It is now 2.20 p.m. and a keen breeze is coming off the river. While Jane washed the dishes I relaxed in the van with a cigarette and wrote this down: such a glorious life it is and I feel like a millionaire. Jane does all the chores as she feels it is enough for me that I do the driving. And of course I agree—gleefully! But now we must be off again for I am anxious to see the "rose coloured" walls of Caerlaverock Castle.

And such a magnificent ruin Caerlaverock is, with a re-constructed drawbridge and water still in the moat, the first time we have ever seen such a thing. There are beautiful mouldings above the doors and portals and a magnificent view from the curtain walls. This mediaeval stronghold was besieged by Edward I of England in 1300 and eventually "dismantled" by the Covenanters in 1640, only six years after reconstruction. Caerlaverock was for centuries the seat of the Maxwell family.

In Annan we purchased a colour spool for our camera and then on to Gretna Green. We had tea with cakes and honey in a big layby just beyond the wedding smithy, near the railway line, where I could watch the trains crossing the border, north and south, and while Jane tidied up I wrote my diary. You just can't afford to let this sort of thing fall behind; you've got to keep at it every day taking notes if you want to get everything in focus. I can't afford to get it on film so I have to get it in writing if I want to preserve a memory of our holidays. Something to look forward to in our old age—should we live that long.

I am always hungry at the wheel, so we fill two big flasks with tea at breakfast to keep us going during the day, and it saves us lighting the stove. I am also smoking 12 to 15 tipped cigarettes a day and I feel that I should have brought my pipe along as well. Thank heaven Jane doesn't smoke.

It is now 6.10 in the evening and our next objective is Hadrian's Wall in Northumberland. Apparently it is futile to look for the Roman Wall either at Carlisle or Newcastle, where they have carted away all the stones to build these cities, so you must turn inland to the mountains, where the wall is less accessible, and where it has been left intact for many miles over the centuries. Now that preservation is in progress it is likely to remain so; safe from the marauding stone thief and a great attraction for the tourists who visit the wall in great numbers every year.

From Brampton we turned left at Blenkinsop level-crossings for the ramparts of the wall at Greenheads, where it can be reached by car and well observed through glasses. At Mile-castle Inn (at the junction to Haltwhistle) we turned left again to Cawfields, where I left Jane in the van and went in search of somewhere to spend the night, some place where we thought we would be safe from strangers. I came upon a family in a caravan near the wall and I asked the gentleman in charge if I could park my van beside them for the night. He said I could do anything I pleased, that the hill didn't belong to him, but when I explained the nature of my request he said it was perfectly all right to muck in with them. He thought we had a tent or something and seemed surprised when I explained that we slept in the small A30 Austin van, but I assured him that we had plenty of room and could manage fine on our own.

After parking the van we went for a walk on the wall and I measured it ten feet across. With the glasses I could see the ramparts of the wall looping for miles over the mountain peaks like an array of toy forts. After dark, with the wall just visible in the waning sky, I lay in the van dreaming about all these early Romans toiling at the wall, cold in this northern outpost of their empire, far from their homes and wives and families, and the Roman soldiers whipping their English slaves carrying and dressing stones for the great wall that was to be a mighty bulwark against the savage hordes who came down from my native Scotland to plunder their settlements. I could see the Picts in their thousands jeering at their efforts and tossing spears at the guards, undaunted by the Roman legions garrisoned in the forts behind the wall. It took something like two-hundred years to build, and in the 400 years of its useful existence the wall was penetrated several times by the Picts. But undoubtedly Hadrian was a master strategist, for nowhere else in Roman Britain could he have chosen a site for the wall more wisely than the great chain of mountains that stretch across Northumbria almost from coast to coast.

July 24th, Sunday

It is raining. I didn't bother to shave but put on my water-proof and went to have another look at the wall. Such a pity it was raining as I had intended walking over a mile of the fortifications, over the higher ramparts, and I got up early to attempt it. Because of the cliffs there is no defensive ditch at Greenheads, but earthworks are in evidence that Roman

45

camps existed as supply bases behind the wall. The ditch I believe was on the north side of the wall, wherever it was necessary, but here I could find no trace of it. Nearer Newcastle, where the road is built on the foundations of the wall the ditch is plainly visible for miles on end.

I gathered up seven fragments of stone as souvenirs and walked back to the van in the rain, sadly disappointed that my pilgrimage had not been more extensive. There was still no sign of anyone from the caravan and obviously they were not so concerned about the Roman Wall as I was, but as Jane had everything packed up for the road we set sail without disturbing anyone.

On the road east to Housesteads we could see the wall on our left, still looping over the cliff-tops and dipping into the valleys, with square forts visible on the hillsides behind the bastion. I lost my way beyond Corbridge and nearly landed in Newcastle. We doubled back within sight of the city and returned to Corbridge to take our bearings. I did admit that I made mistakes and this was one of them, where I got mixed up with my road numbers in a network of junctions. Ah well, there is only one thing for it to keep our schedule straight, and that is to skip Flodden battlefield on the way home, much to my regret, for I have wept for Flodden since my schooldays and yearned to see it since reading Scott's "Marmion". Another time perhaps we shall see it.

At Corbridge the rain was dancing on the streets and we were glad to seek shelter in the souvenir shops, where I bought a booklet on Hadrian's Wall, and several postcards, which we wrote in the van, posted in the rain and then ran helter skelter for the public conveniences.

It was still pelting when we left Corbridge, the windscreen wipers splashing it aside in great swaths of water. Later it became more fitful, with patches of pale green sun on the hills and quiffs of loosened rain hanging from the clouds. And thus north to Jedburgh by the A68 on switch-back scenic-railway roads at speeds that lift your stomach in the dips and traffic to make your head swim. There were flocks of cyclists on the road, slicing on in the rain in coloured shorts. I became hungry again so we stopped for tea by the roadside at 11.35 a.m.; in a layby of course, for I never park a car in traffic.

46

Now over the Cheviot Hills to the border, where we stopped to have a look round the rolling hills with the glasses, even as far north as the Eildons. The sun was now making a patchwork quilt of the landscape, flooding the valleys with his light and casting cloud shadows on the hills, fleeting silhouettes that were caught in his powerful lenses. As we sped along I caught a glimpse of Ferniehurst Castle among the trees on my right, a mere glimpse on the road to Jedburgh. Here I tried in vain to take a picture of the ruined abbey, but the sun was too fitful. So we bought postcards and lettered rock and strolled round the town.

I looked in at the cinema where carpenters were at work in the hall, either repairing it or transforming it to something else. I couldn't be sure because the screen was still in position while several rows of chairs were missing at the front. I was going to enquire what the men were about on a Sunday but Jane said my curiosity was getting out of hand and pulled me back. We bought a postcard of Queen Mary's House and looked at Prince Charlie's Lodgings on a side-street. Jedburgh Castle was closed for renovation, so we left the town and off to have dinner by the roadside: boiled potatoes and tinned soup, prunes, cake and tea, and the sun shining on my page again as I write. It is now after four in the afternoon and I am drowsy with content and a full belly.

I bought three more gallons of petrol at a garage near Selkirk (the last was at Brampton) and now 4d. more a gallon in Wilson's emergency budget to beat inflation. I didn't know this for lack of newspapers or a car radio but the woman at the pump had to inform me of the new prices. Whisky and beer also up and wages to be frozen and many other restrictions to be imposed to try and bolster our faltering economy. But Mr. Wilson was clever enough to raise his own salary, and that of his colleagues immediately he came to power, probably because he knew this was going to happen. All the same I blame the shipping strike more than Wilson, and all those other stupid strikes that the rest of us have got to pay for. You can't blame the Labour Government for everything that has befallen us since they came to power, and some of the workers haven't given them a chance really. It looks to me that the Unions have tied Labour's hands behind his back, and that they will

47

remain tied until he gets kicked out of office again, unless somebody kicks the Unions out. But who dares . . .?

Through Selkirk to Peebles with a spatter of rain on the windscreen. I was somewhat disconsolate because I was unshaved and toothless and I had burst the zipper in front of my trousers. I had to keep pulling down my jersey and have my jacket fastened when I left the van in the towns. We have been in these border towns before, around 1960, when we slept a night in our Hillman car in the public park at Hawick, because we hadn't a tent and we couldn't find bed and breakfast. In any case it was a delightful holiday, one of our first since the children grew up, and our first in a car of our own, though I have no record of it in my diaries. But I remember being greatly taken with Mungo Park's monument at Selkirk though I have not seen his birthplace.

Today, about two miles beyond Peebles I drew into the roadside to look at Neidpath Castle. It is perched on a dominant crag high above a graceful bend in the Tweed. We left the van and walked through a wicket in the dyke, down the avenue of trees on the grassy slope to the castle. We stood on the bank overlooking the river, with the grim walls of the castle towering above us, impressive and overpowering, but the treble of the water and the beauty and silence of the trees changed the picture to one of utter bliss and serenity. The castle was closed at this advanced hour, for it was near seven in the evening, but we were content to walk round the landward side to view the great tower and the surrounding beauty. The path on the riverside was a mere ledge on the cliff-top, and the very sight of it made me feel like a beetle on a wall, and we drew back from it with swimming heads. An old woman stood in the castle door, mumbling something to an old man on a stick, while he hobbled over to the dyke and fixed a bar across the open gate, just to let us know he wasn't letting us in. The formidable building, the eerie, silent atmosphere and the old man and woman at the gate was like that part of a dream when you are about to enter a fairyland of surprises—and then you wake up and all has vanished. On a notice board at the roadside I could see that the ancient castle belonged to a Property Syndicate but was open to the public at certain hours. I motored round the bend and looked back at Neidpath

48

through the trees, from where you mostly see it in illustrations from Scott, and even without a signpost I believe I would have guessed its identity. I have long wished to see Neidpath and now I have been rewarded, all the more so as we came upon it by surprise, for I had little idea of where it was situated.

We motored on to Blyth Bridge and Newbigging on the A721, beyond Carstairs, where we forked right on the A706 as far as the village of Forth, and a mile beyond, where we slept the night on a Lanark coalfield.

July 25th, Monday

This is quite the most depressing and unromantic spot we have ever awakened in. It was almost dark when we settled in but now we could see that we were surrounded by giant slag heaps, disused mine shafts, with moor and cotton grass to the mists on the horizon. The little town of Forth a mile to the south was our nearest contact with Civilisation. But we were close beside the main road and the traffic and this had given us heart to stay here for the night.

This is the only time it had been a little cold in the van, so we filled a hot-water bottle between us and soon fell asleep until morning, when I discovered we had slept the night on a recent subsidence, which had been filled up with rubble, but the ground shook violently with every passing lorry. And all around us the wild empty moor, and the occasional baa of a sheep in the darkness. Now it was daylight I could see an old smoke stack quite near us, some ruined brick buildings and a derelict farm house. I ran my glasses over this panorama of social history. A shepherd was moving his flock among the grass-grown slag heaps and I could hear the sharp bark of his dog. I brought the smoke stack into close focus, a column of crumbling brick pointing at the sky and I searched the deserted mine workings rusting in the sun, the uprooted railway tracks, the miners' cottages, forsaken and blackened with smog, and I reflected on the days past when women and children must have burrowed under our feet, toiling with the men for a few pence a day, labouring for the black diamonds that made Britain Great as an industrial nation, the sweat and

49

child labour that built the stately homes of England; the wealth that made tyrants, the slavery that created the slums and the Trade Unions, the power that built the greatest empire of the nineteenth century, the coal that provided the motive power for our factories, for our railways, and for our battleships—and now it was all at my feet, a shamble of weeds and neglect.

Presently a man stopped his car on the road and asked the way to Darvel. I couldn't direct him but I gave him a look at my map. Then a milk lorry stopped and I bought a pint of milk and six rolls from the driver, who then directed the stranger to Darvel, birthplace of Sir Alexander Fleming, who discovered penicillin.

Once on the road again I bought a pint of oil at Breicht, where the woman at the filling station told me that since the mines closed down grass had grown on the slag bings and stopped the smog. The air was cleaner she said. Only two mines were still working and she pointed to a huge black pyramid freshly erupted and mounted with modern machinery, a long escalator right to the top of the ramp, and a cableway of buckets that took the coal straight to the railhead. The refuse was being used for roadmaking.

We stopped for shopping at Armadale. It is always best to stop in the small towns on holiday; this too we have learned from excruciating experience. The service is admittedly slower but you don't have the crowds and you don't have to carry the purchases because you can usually get the car right to the shop, especially so in the morning. We took two colour prints in the grounds of the Barnardo Institute at Falkirk and had tea by the roadside at Denny.

And thus on to Stirling and the field of Bannockburn, a name that has blazed in my memory in letters of fire since my schooldays, when it was my mental playground; and now I was standing on the field for the first time in reality, where I know that Bruce had faced the might of Edward, and my pilgrimage was amply rewarded. And such a wonderful statue they have erected there to the King of Scots, mounted on his warhorse (or is it the palfrey on which he faced De Buhne?) with battleaxe in hand, addressing his troops before the battle. Wallace and Bruce were the heroes of my boyhood and here in

Stirling I could find them both, so we motored through the city to the Abbey Craig, where we parked the van and walked up to the Wallace Monument. Such was my enthusiasm—and Jane's companionship—that we climbed to the topmost parapets of the monument, 520 feet above sea level, and looked at central Scotland through our glasses. We were not at all sure that we could do it, and we bought our admission tickets with quaking hearts, but with a good rest on the first and second floors we finally made it. I suppose they have placed the Wallace sword on the second floor in case it is too much for some people to reach the top landing; but for us it was a challenge and we climbed on to the top of the monument. If anyone thinks this is a small feat let him have a crack at it himself and see, especially if he is over 50 and is prepared to climb something nearly twice the height of the Scott Monument in Edinburgh, from sea level. But it sickened us to see a father holding his toddler son over the ledge for kicks.

It was a beautiful day and the glasses brought the colours into deep focus, like Todd—AO on the big screen, and the first view had all the breathless beauty in the opening scenes of that wonderful film "The Sound of Music", when the Panavision camera sweeps you over the mountain vistas of the Austrian Tyrol, deep and heart-clutching in their frightening splendour. On the west over the city I could pick out Ben Lomond, Ben Ledi and I believe Ben Vorlich, in that order moving north, and on the south the Links of Forth; to the east the river estuary and Forth Bridges, not forgetting the Seven Battlefields, though I looked for only three: Sheriffmuir, Bannockburn and Stirling Bridge. Here was the most spectacular view we had ever seen, or ever likely to see again, and also all the relics inside the tower, including the collection of paintings on the exploits of Wallace, a history lesson in itself if one had time to linger on them. Besides all this there was a tinker playing the bag-pipes at the base of the crag, providing the right atmosphere, especially I suppose for our American visitors, and judging by the way some of the German girls were regaling the statue of Bruce at Bannockburn.

We were a shilling for our admission, one-and-sixpence for postcards, a sixpence for a guide-book, a shilling for ice-cream and threepence to the tinker, five-shillings and three-pence for the crowning glory of our holiday; for a finale in grandeur and coloured spectacle we shall never really forget.

In the Fair City of Perth I bought a pair of light dress trousers to replace the ones I wore. I put them on in the fitting room and the assistant parcelled my old pair in brown paper. The trews cost me £3. 4/-, reduced from £3. 9/- at John Collier's and I am delighted with them.

Three more gallons of petrol at Coupar Angus and a fish and chip supper at Forfar, tea at Grandma's at Stonehaven and we arrived home safely at 12.15 a.m. on Tuesday, July 26th when it was quite dark. But there were lights in our windows for Graham was not yet in bed. With 18 gallons of petrol we had covered about 700 miles and spent roughly £15, excluding my new trousers. We had slept five nights in the open, which would have cost us at least £9 in bed-and-breakfast fees, so this much we saved with the van.

July 29th, Friday

Today we motored to the Priory at Pluscarden, six miles west of Elgin, in Morayshire, which must be about 70 miles from our home, and therefore no mean pilgrimage. But such a rewarding visit it proved to be and such a beautiful setting for the monastery. Nestling serenely in the green valley, beneath the steeply wooded hills to the north, this Benedictine sanctuary lies metaphorically in the green pastures and quiet waters of the scriptural church. Here indeed is a pleasant valley, secluded and peaceful, and the priory such a surprise to be found here, like some fairyland wonder of childhood suddenly become a reality.

We bought berries from the monks, supplied from their huge walled garden: strawberries, raspberries and blackberries for jam-making, 2/6 to 3/- a pound; clean, fresh, and of very good quality. A host of visitors were shown over the reconstruction work by the monks, detailing the ecclesiastical history of the older building and the features and scope of the restoration. These monks wear a white habit in cloister and I was surprised to learn that of the 19 brothers in residence only one is a builder to trade; the others are carpenters, sculptors, potters, painters and artists in stained glass, activities which are practised in the monastery precincts, but the task of rebuilding the church to its former dimensions is contracted to firms in Elgin as funds will allow. Even the great rose window in the north transept, which is 16 feet in diameter was executed by outside craftsmen at a cost of £5,000. This window depicts the woman and the serpent from the Book of Revelation and is beautifully done in vivid colours. Set at a great height in the wall it looks no bigger than a town clock, but one of the monks assured us that its circumference would allow the entry of a double-decker bus, which I thought was an adept description for the layman. The ultimate completion of the abbey to its former glory, prior to its destruction by the Wolf of Badenoch in 1390, may occupy a period of 50 to 100 years. Novices come and go and the dormitories are equipped with modern conveniences, even to ash-trays on the tables, which surprised me considerably in this house of the crucifix and candles, incense and prayer. The monks have a tractor, and although they grow a few acres of barley and potatoes they don't seem to keep a cow—judging by the amount of bottled milk stacked in crates by the kitchen doors.

But next time you read in the papers that the monks of Pluscarden (pronounced Pluscardene) are rebuilding their abbey—well, don't you believe it, as I was bold enough to find out, by asking how many of them were builders. And don't be deceived by the hooded monk building the dyke at the entrance. He is the only master builder among the brothers and he has been at that dyke for quite a while, a little bit at a time to make it last, and to impress the likes of you and me.

Within the abbey grounds there is a Catholic graveyard, where some of the brothers and a few parishioners have been interred, and simple wooden crosses mark the graves.

Thus to Spynie Palace, near Lossiemouth, the one time palatial residence of the Bishops of Moray, with whom Badenoch quarrelled before he set fire to Elgin Cathedral and Pluscarden. The main square tower is of enormous dimensions, with walls on the defensive side nearly twelve feet thick, with ornamented turret bases on the roofless gables, indicating a castellated tower-keep of tremendous height and strength, and the courtyard about an acre square, with three smaller towers at the blank corners of the great curtain wall, which drops sheer in the north to the Lossie canal, the whole structure enclosed in a copse of trees with only the main tower conspicuous from the Elgin-Lossie road, as it was at one time from the railway behind it, which has now gone.

Jane took my picture in a ruined archway of the curtain wall at the Bishop's Palace, which typifies my quest for these ruined structures from a bygone age. And I was pleased to note that restoration work to the great tower of the palace is in progress, preserving an important landmark in our ecclesiastical history. From Hadrian's Wall in Northumberland to Pluscarden in Moray, and the Wallace Monument at Stirling in between, all within a week—surely this isn't bad going for an amateur antiquarian in archaelogical survey.

This is Ramsay MacDonald country and he lies buried near the Palace of Spynie, where no doubt he played as a boy, and the small cottage which was his childhood home is still preserved in Lossiemouth.

But the most romantic of my discoveries for the day was the shell of Duffus Castle across the road from Lossiemouth airfield. Perched on a green mound which looks like a former motte, and probably at one time surrounded by a moat, Duffus to me resembled a precious stone set in emerald, a royal jewel embedded in green plush, symbol of a secret past and guardian of a history of which I am so far ignorant, except for the general belief that this was where Macbeth, as the Thane of Glamis stabbed King Duncan, though I have heard the same claim for Cawdor Castle, and even for Inverness, and Glamis. Tradition names four sites for the murder of King Duncan, by Macbeth, but with "a heath near Forres" in such close proximity I should think that Cawdor or Duffus have the stronger claim.

Once a royal stronghold, Duffus now stands wild and uncivilised, the broken mirror of a distant past, in stark contrast to this arable and fertile plain of Moray. Yet it was from this gaunt and lonely ruin that the name of Moray originated. It was granted as a fief to a Flemish soldier of fortune, one Freskin de Moravia, for services rendered to the Scottish crown, and by this means also we inherited the name of Murray. By the thirteenth century the family became known as the House of Moray, with great power in the land.

54

Eventually, by marriage Duffus passed to the Cheynes, who were staunch Royalists in the Scottish Wars of Independence, which brought about the downfall of the castle. Like Skelbo Castle on the Dornoch Firth, Duffus is uniquely associated with the ill-fated Maid of Norway. In 1290 it was visited by the commissioners of Edward I of England on their way to Kirkwall to greet the Maid, as a bride for his son, and also on their return from Skelbo with the sad tidings of her drowning, perhaps having seen her corpse.

The Cheynes died out in the middle of the fourteenth century and Duffus reverted to a descendant of the original House of Freskin, in the person of Nicholas, son of the fourth Earl of Sutherland, who is credited with the building of the great stone tower of Duffus, which replaced the earlier timber fort. From sheer weight over the centuries the stonework slipped down the motte and now leans drunkenly against it, and it is this towering symbol of despair which gives to Duffus Castle its character and chapter in Scottish history. The mound originally covered an area of from eight to ten acres.

1967

April 22nd, Saturday

A morning shrouded in snow but all gone by dinner-time in the bright sun.

Today I had my first run as solo driver in our new car, our Vauxhall Viva de Luxe. Well it isn't exactly new; a year old and one previous owner with only 12,000 miles on the clock, immaculate condition and cost us £560, plus the £100 we got in part exchange for our German NSU, which was giving us a spot of bother, and Graham was the only one of our sons who could drive it. That such luxury should be ours exceeds my fondest dreams, thanks to our benevolent minded oldest son, who put up most of the money to let us have it. We have a tent now as well, which we bought second-hand for £7 from the advertisement columns in the local paper; blue Canadian type, with a centre pole, two gauze windows, porch canopy, ground-sheet attached, pegs and guyropes, the whole thing easily assembled for packing in the car boot, and just as easily erected on a new site. So now we have tent will travel.

In the meantime I had Jane in the front beside me and Grandma in the back seat and we drove down to Fraserburgh, where I bought an ounce of black twist and walked up to the old Picture House, now a Bingo Hall, in Mid Street. This was one of the shrines of my youth, a glorified dream house where I saw my fondest visions. Thence to Rosehearty and tea from our flasks near the ruins of Pitsligo Castle (1603), with the shattered outline of Pittulie Castle just across the fields. At New Pitsligo village I went into St. John's Episcopal Church, a beautifully pillared building with fine windows in stained glass, and there I read from Chronicles II, Chapter 6, of Solomon's building a great house to the glory of God. "Now, my God, let, I beseech thee, thine eyes be open, and let thine ears be attent unto the prayer that is made in this place." Which perhaps was my expression of thankfulness for being spared alive and well on this wonderful day.

June 25th, Sunday

A beautiful day, we stopped the car in the village of Cults, on the north Deeside road from Aberdeen, and walked into the church of Saint Devenick, about six miles from the city. St. Devenick was buried in the area and here I give my own translation of THE BURIAL OF SAINT DEVENICK from Barbour's LEGENDS OF THE SAINTS, which more or less confirms this belief.

> But they that the corpse brought thither,
> With it had gone their way together
> Nearby of Crostan to the hill,
> And there abade, to rest at will.
> But Saint Machar in his quest,
> Followed and found them there take rest.
> And he and his three with them stayed
> Till they the service all had made;
> That for such deed men should devise
> Or any sleep come near their eyes.
> And then they bore the corpse devoutly
> Unto a place called Banchory.
> And there solemnly with honour
> They gathered for it a sepulchre.
> And on him there they made a kirk,
> Where God yet ceases not from work—
> But through prayer for all he feels
> And sick and sair folk gladly heals;
> Men calls that place where the saint lay
> Banchory—Devenyk till this day.

And so they do. We may further assume that Crostan got its name from the fact that the followers of the saint rested on the hill, and set up a cross by the bier while they waited for Saint Machar. We found the present church impressive but plainer than we expected and only three windows in coloured glass.

July 9th, Sunday

We did 129 miles in the Viva. We had tea by the roadside at Kildrummy Church, and again on the grass at Corgarf. I was not impressed with the old fortress of Corgarf, only with its history. A beautiful day with a soft hot wind and gorgeous scenery. Jane always on the hunt for flowers. Anything growing in a ditch or by the roadside—if it seems that it would look equally well in our garden it has to be transported forthwith. The place is overcrowded but still she brings them home. Six years ago I tore up a Lilac bush from the roadside between Montrose and Forfar and planted it in our garden. Six years ago and not a flower has appeared on it yet, nothing but leaves, not even a bud. And twice I have transplanted the thing: first because it was too near the gate, secondly because it was too near the dyke and the cows took a fancy to it, and now it merely survives where it gets all the bitter blasts that blow, and that means something here I can tell you. Oh yes and we have two kinds of Ivy creeping up the walls and wrapping itself around the gateposts: we have a variety from Gight Castle with very tiny leaves and a sprig from Mill of Tifty that looks like taking possession of the place. And Jane knows every flower and where it came from, honestly or otherwise, and they remind her of every place we have visited and the many happy hours we have spent in the car. These little flower beds are Jane's scrap-books of memory, her living memorials of past joys.

Oh yes, and I must tell you about the little yellow cress that was growing in the roof-gutter of an old deserted farm-workers cottage down in Angus. She spotted the thing as I went flashing past and she had me stop the car and reverse back to have a look at it. She had been looking for this yellow-eyed thing for years and now here it was for the taking. The windows of the cottage were curtained in sack cloth and there was no smoke from the chimneys, so I got out of the car and lifted a length of the creeper from the rone. It was moist like moss and the roots shaped as the gutter it filled, about half an arm's length of the stuff, and I put it in the car. Grandma was with us and she wanted a strip as well, and I had just grabbed this and was taking it down from the rone when an old man opened the door and looked straight into my face. We both stared at each other and I didn't even have the presence of mind to ask the way to some outlandish place—just threw the flower in the car and made off as fast as I could get into gear. It was a good laugh but all you "Flower People" beware of those seemingly deserted cottages, and whoever may be watching you from behind the cobwebbed window panes.

August 9th, Wednesday

Holiday in Lakeland!

We left home in the Viva at 9 a.m. Ran into rain between Brechin and Forfar, and extremely heavy rain approaching Perth. Skies overcast and the hills dark with rain clouds. We stopped in Lanark where Jane went shopping. I was meanwhile intrigued by what remained of the old Rio Cinema in the town's Castlegate, a few blocks down from the site of the house of Sir William Wallace, marked by a plaque on the wall, which informs us that Wallace (born at Elderslie, near Paisley) first drew the sword here for Scotland, when he slew an English soldier who provoked him to fight, and was declared an outlaw.

I went inside the old picture house, only the frontage remaining intact, and an old woman told me that this too is due for demolition. The Rio is truly Spanish in design; not unlike our old Casino Cinema that used to stand in Wales Street, Aberdeen—now the Boulevard. But the main hall of the Rio had been destroyed by fire, and the vestibule still remained full of rubble and charred, blackened wood, and the paintwork blistered on the walls. The box-office was still intact and the peep-holes in the wall of the projection room. I just couldn't resist a place like this: a dreamhouse in a shambles, no doubt still the home of memories for a great many people. But a murder had just been committed in a graveyard outside the town and I was afraid that the murderer might be lurking somewhere in this ruined building, in this rubble, so I retraced my steps and went to look for Jane.

The rain had cleared somewhat so we drove off and pitched our tent in a caravan site at Crawford, north of Beattock, on the main road to Carlisle, which is extremely busy; what with the road at our backs and the railway in front of us we hardly slept a wink. Here I saw for the first time one of the new freight-liner trains speeding south at tremendous speed. It was heartening to think that such new vibrant life had come to the railways, and that maybe after all Dr. Beeching could be forgiven for his ruthless curtailment of the branch lines.

But they shouldn't allow dogs on camping sites. Here I had to remove the unmentionable before I could pitch our tent.

August 10th, Thursday

We got up early and packed our gear and motored to Ecclefechan, just off the main road and stopped to look at the house where Thomas Carlyle was born, December 4th, 1795. We arrived at 9 a.m. and couldn't wait for the house to open, so we bought a picture postcard of it and motored back up the brae to see Carlyle's statue, where he sits on a chair, in contemplative mood, oh so naturally, in cast iron, overlooking the village of his birth, with his face towards England. At this time of the morning, while the village was not yet fully awake, this peep into its past had an eerie feeling of curiosity and excitement.

Our next stop was at Bruce's Cave at Dunskelly Manor House, Kirkpatrick, family seat of the Irvines, descendants of the King's standard-bearer at Bannockburn, while an Irvine of Drum, Aberdeenshire, was his armour-bearer, members of the same family. Is this then the cave of the spider fable? Are we beholding the site of our schoolboy wonder? Nobody could tell me for certain but the cave is impressive high up on the cliff wall overlooking the wooded Kirtle river.

We had dinner in a layby just over the border, and then through Carlisle to Keswick, where, in Crosthwaite churchyard I located the grave and mausoleum of poet-laureate Robert Southey. Little did I dream, thirty years ago, when I read THE LIFE OF NELSON, that I should one day stand beside the grave of its author; and I have to thank the Brazilian Government, not my own countrymen, not even Englishmen for restoring it in 1961, because Southey had published a History of Brazil in 1813.

We went inside the ancient fourteenth-century church with its square Norman tower and two rows of massive pillars supporting the roof. We walked along the aisle to the far end where there is a marble effigy of Southey on a bier. He lived for 40 years in Keswick and died there on March 21st, 1843.

Southey was not a truly great poet, but out of all his industry
he left us a little gem called THE BATTLE OF BLENHEIM, which
most of us remember from our school-days, and for this at least
we must revere him:

> With fire and sword the country round
> Was wasted far and wide,
> And many a childing mother then,
> And new-born infant died.
> But things like that, you know, must be
> At every famous victory.

Hugh Walpole also lies in Keswick, in St. John's churchyard,
but it slipped my memory and I was pressed for time, otherwise
I would have looked for his grave, though I have never read
his novels. He lived for a time at nearby Brakenburn, where he
did much of his work and died there on June 1st, 1941.

There is a theatre in Keswick called The Century, and when
I looked at their play-dates I was astounded to find they were
going to perform THE RIVALS, by Richard Brinsley Sheridan,
a play I had enjoyed reading many years ago but thought
nobody would risk running it nowadays. In this respect
Keswick resembles Pitlochry in Scotland, which also boasts a
"Theatre in the Hills", which, but for the Arts Council, would
hardly be possible in these small towns, when we can scarcely
support a "live" theatre in places the size of Aberdeen or
Perth.

It was a lovely day in Keswick and the curio shops were a
sheer delight. I like the postcard racks with their kaleidoscope
of coloured views, and those linen dishcloths with a map of the
local countryside, its history and its beauty spots, for I believe
that these things heighten the holiday spirit and they never
fail to excite me with expectancy. But here there were tubs of
flowers on the pavements and lashings of blue and orange
hydrangeas against the white walls. There were purple
mountains behind the housetops where sun-spot gilded the
colours of bracken, rock and scree. Beauty, history and poetry,
the breath of my being; three of my reasons for living, and here
I was in a surfeit.

Wherever you open your eyes in Lakeland you look upon
beauty: it would be a dull eye that couldn't perceive it; every

61

vista an artist's dream, a poet's paradise, and the effect upon the mind is one of mild rapture and a strange delight.

Jane bought some small gifts and we had tea in the car park and sped on to still lovelier Grasmere, where I was enchanted with the Wordsworth Cottage, the museum across the road, and the churchyard of St. Olav, where Wordsworth sleeps with his family, all of which we visited before nightfall.

Dove Cottage, in the vale of Grasmere, for nine years the home of William and Dorothy Wordsworth. To think that I stood in the actual room where Dorothy wrote her delightful Journal; that I was looking on the same scenes she describes so beautifully, and that I was reading the poems (under glass) almost on the spot where Wordsworth had written them—it was all so entrancing and beyond my fondest hopes only a few years back. My cup was overflowing, my heart was full; some of my dearest ambitions had been fulfilled and I felt smugly satisfied that I had lived to achieve it.

The sun was still in ambient glory when we pitched our tent on a grassy bank overlooking Grasmere Lake, an alpine valley enclosed by sunswept hills and stately pines, where we looked across to the wooded island and its boathouse, the village and its church tower, and up the sky-blue valley between majestic Silver Howe and Dunmail Raise, and the road back to Keswick twisting over the mountains. The lake was like a negative of trembling reflections, where even a fly would have made a splash on its limpid surface.

We leased our pitch from Mrs. J. Fawcett, of Dale End Farm for 4/- a night, milk at a shilling a pint and eggs at 4/6d. a dozen, and because the weather broke later on we were glad to get in.

August 11th, Friday

This morning we discovered we had a burst silencer and we were informed that we wouldn't get it repaired anywhere nearer than Windermere. So we drove there in a slashing rain storm and the thunder crashing all around us. Blue lightning was splitting the darkened sky, slicing into the blinding rain in deep, livid sword-thrusts of quivering light. To say that Jane was frightened is putting it mildly. She was nearly frantic, and because it was so difficult to observe the signposts in the storm, and I had to leave the car so often to ask the way I was nearly soaked. What with the rain and the roar of the broken silencer, flying on through every village you would have thought I was in a racing car hell bent for glory.

After a frustrating search we found the Vauxhall garage in a back street, only to be told they couldn't look at us until afternoon, and we joined the queue of cars awaiting repairs. But I told the foreman of the plight we were in, and so far from home, on such a day as this, with all our cooking utensils left in the tent at Grasmere—so at last he relented and a mechanic took the Viva from us and drove it into the garage.

There was nothing for it but wait, so we wandered about the town and took photographs in the blinks of sun between the showers. With most of our provisions left in the tent, or in the boot of the car, and having spent so much on these already, we felt we couldn't afford to have a meal in a restaurant (something we seldom have in any case) far less an hotel, so by way of dinner we had fish and chips and ate them in a doorway, to be out of the rain. Later we bought postcards and wrote them to friends at home from the reading-room of the Public Library.

Car ready by 3 o'clock: cost us £3, plus 5/- tip to the foreman for having it done. By now the rain had cleared and the sun had come out, so we drove to Bowness and along the shores of Lake Windermere, almost to Newby Bridge, but turned back to AMBLE in Ambleside. And such a beautiful little town with its painted houses and roses round the doors, flowers on the dykes and on every niche that would hold them; masses of mauve clematis clinging to the white walls and tubs of flowers on the sidewalks.

And a word here about the houses and cottages of Lakeland: wherever you turn, in village or country lane, they have a character all their own; built with those grey-green slate stones almost without mortar or visible cement, which gives a tremendous impression of symmetrical perfection, approaching an art, and sun after rain softens the colours into satin, spiced with gold and silver. And the round built stone chimneys, without pots or cans, but spiked slates topped with a flat stone, probably to induce draught in pulling the smoke up the flue, or to keep out the rain from dripping trees. Whatever the reason of these chimneys it adds to the individuality of the Lakeland cottages as being different from anything I have ever seen before.

August 12th, Saturday

Back to shopping in Keswick: more postcards, pictures and curios, and an atmosphere gilded with sunshine; veils of mist creeping up the mountains and sun-spot seeking out the colours of heather, rock and tree. I bought the poems of James Russell Lowell, the American poet in four volumes for two bob at a charity sale, searching out the books separately from the jumble on the counters, which took me no more than five minutes in spite of the crowd, for I have a quick eye for book titles.

Later we drove through Whinlatter Pass to Loweswater, Crumnock Water and Buttermere. We had dinner on the hillside in Honister Pass, near a rollicking burn and a serpentine road. Jane took my picture seated on a rock, like a statue, reading a book, and I took her preparing our dinner on the gas stove. In Borrowdale we went inside the tiny hillside chapel, white and lonely in this silent, beautiful valley.

Here I talked to a farmer in his yard about the local breed of Herdwick sheep. He took me into a barn and showed me the fleeces, black the first year and getting lighter year by year as the animals get older. The Herdwick looks like something between a goat and the Blackface-Cross, unlike any animal I have ever seen before (unless it were Jacob's lambs at Scone Palace), but they are sure-footed and agile in their hardy scramble for subsistence on the craggy mountainsides. The breeding of Herdwick sheep was greatly encouraged by Miss Beatrix Potter, who eventually owned the greater part of the Lake district, which she bequeathed at her death to the National Trust.

The farmer I talked to had three names for the mountain peak behind his farm-house. He said he had been up there three times that week gathering sheep for the weaning, and I could only marvel at his pluck for a man over 60, because it was more than I had stomach for. Coming down from Honister Pass was enough for me, like sliding down the roof on a church tower. We drove up the shore of Derwent Water to Keswick, the only way back, I was told, and thus "home" to Grasmere, where it was again raining merrily, playing a tune on the tin-cans in the bin yard.

August 13th, Sunday

Today we went to Coniston, and of all the people in the village I was fortunate in asking the whereabouts of the Ruskin Museum from a woman whose father had been gardener to John Ruskin for many years at Brantwood Manor, high up on the shores of Coniston Water. She was on her way home from church, an old spinster dressed in blue and carrying her bible and umbrella, and she said she had spent her life as a children's nanny. I could have asked dozens of others on the street, but she was the one ordained that I should meet. She wouldn't give me her name but said she remembered Ruskin as a very quiet and humble man with great kindness of heart, which she believed was common with all really clever people. She had never spoken to the great man but as a girl she remembered his funeral, when he had lain in state for five days in Coniston Church, with six great candles burning beside his bier, from January 20th to the 25th, 1900. Her father, she added, had lived to be ninety.

Later, at the Museum, we had a terrible fight with the turnstile, which refused to let us inside, no matter how many pennies I dropped into the slot. Eventually I lost patience with the thing and climbed over the top of it, but left Jane standing out in the cold. Some more visitors arrived however and got the thing to work, so she got inside with them, while I was still engrossed with the exhibits. Here we saw the giant candlesticks which were used at Ruskin's funeral, besides his geological hammer and innumerable rock specimens; examples of his handwriting; books, pictures, etc., all under glass, and a picture of the great man in flowing beard at his desk in the study at Brantwood.

When we left the museum we walked along the village streets to look at Ruskin's gravestone in the churchyard, a masterpiece of scuplture in the Celtic tradition of stone carving.

We afterwards went to Coniston Water, where Donald

Campbell was killed in his speed-boat Bluebird, on the 4th January this year. It was also in the vicinity of Coniston that Von Werra escaped from a prisoner-of-war camp for Germans and later wrote his book, "The One That Got Away". We didn't have time to visit Ruskin's home at Brantwood, but next year I am determined to do so.

If ever I had any childhood ideals of Fairyland surely these were realised at Hawkshead, an image which was strengthened by magical names like The Minstrel's Gallery and Ann Tyson's Cottage, and by the number of Beatrix Potter's Little People displayed on the shelves of the curio shops, where there was also a beechnut house for Snow White and her Seven Dwarfs, about the size of my own head, lit with tiny electric bulbs, and I peered into it with a searching eye. This display was in The Minstrel's Gallery, and of course Ann Tyson's Cottage is where Wordsworth lodged while attending the local Grammar School.

For thruppence each we were permitted inside the old Grammar School, and we were shown where Wordsworth had carved his name on the desk where he studied. The wooden desks are a mass of name carving but Wordsworth's inscription is under glass, much the same as Burns' signature, scratched by the poet in an idle moment with his signet ring on a window pane in the house where he lived in Dumfries.

This was a long way from Ardallie, in Aberdeenshire, where in the little roadside school Jane had learned by heart the sweet sad song of "Lucy Grey", had almost shed tears for her fate in the snow, and where Jane had learned to love the "dancing daffodils"; but she had never really probed the mystery of their originator, merely trusting him as a sort of God with a universal gift for prattling childhood; but now when she realised that he sat in a little country school, much like her own, it shattered a childhood illusion. Perhaps it were better for some of us that we never traced the source of our inspiration; never sought the shrine of our adulation, but remained content as it were to worship from afar. Not that this has in any way impaired Jane's love for Wordsworth, or for his "host of golden daffodils". On the contrary, it became a sharing of identity, for it brought the God of infinity, the mysterious God of her childhood imagination, down to earth, down to her own level

66

of simplicity and understanding, which might be a good thing after all—like Christ on earth.

Also under glass was a seventeenth-century book on forestry by diarist John Evelyn, which I never expected to see in my lifetime, or even suspected its existence still in print; and examples of the early work of Pope and Milton were also on display.

We also visited the magnificent fifteenth-century church with its Norman tower and dovecot gateway. Inside are the table tomb and effigies of the Sandys family, whose ancestor, Edwin Sandys, Archbishop of York, founded Hawkshead Grammar School in 1588.

Next to Beatrix Potter's Hill Top farm-house at New Sawrey, where we were both intrigued with the period furnishings and her original drawings in water-colour.

Until the recent publication of her secret diary, and my reading the review of it in the press, I have never heard much of Beatrix Potter, but now I was here in the quaint old farm-house where she sketched a great many of her animal characters, I was fascinated with the wealth of detail each picture on the walls revealed. Now I can understand her popularity with children, and her little coloured books of animals are every-where. Indeed I wonder whether the late Walt Disney ever visited Hill Top Farm, or what he would have thought of it if he had; there is such a strong resemblance in their work one can't help making a comparison; indeed I would go further and say that Walt Disney merely animated what Beatrix Potter had already originated in still life: not that this made Disney's task any easier, which was essentially a technical one, besides being artistic, but he took the animal character a stage further, a stage nearer human life, nearer the character it was meant to represent, much to the benefit of all of us who admire art in its various forms. Moreover, it was something that had to wait for the twentieth century, with its advanced aids to optical illusion, and has left us with the animated film cartoon.

We drove away from Hill Top farm highly exhilarated, and with each breath drew in the fresh beauty of the trees and lakes and hills of New Sawrey and Hawkshead, which had seemed a fairyland come true. We stopped and had our late dinner in a layby beside one of the beautiful Tarns of Lakeland, a long strip of light blue rippling water and the reeds just showing above the surface, and the trees standing all around gracefully admiring themselves in the shadowed waters. For Jane and me this was like another honeymoon, and we laughed and smiled in each other's faces with the joy of renewed youth. What with our family up and a lot of our troubles behind us perhaps we had occasion to rejoice, thankful that we had yet been spared to each other, and whatever the future held for us we would face together, unified and inspired by these wonderful memories of holidays spent together just like these. So we packed our utensils and drove back in the evening sunshine to our delightful Grasmere.

August 14th, Monday

It rained all morning and Grasmere Lake was barely visible in the lowering clouds. Except for a hurried dash in the car to Grasmere for provisions we sat in the tent or the car most of the day, reading or watching the veils of blue mist rising on the mountainsides. At times almost all was obliterated, save the island and its boathouse and a patch of grey lake around it. I'm sure that the Wordsworths must have seen the lake many times in this mood, for it is an area of quick weather changes and fierce rain storms, but mostly they describe it in summer dress. But our tent was still dry, and except for a wet patch on the canvas around the door, not a drop of rain came through on us. We were pitched on a slope, and while others dug a trench around their tents to divert the water it seeped under our polythene groundsheet with no ill effect to us inside. The people in the next tent on our left thought that we were Welsh from our manner of speaking; they said they were listening to us talking and couldn't make out a word of our language, even though Jane is a very clear speaker, so I told them in English that we conversed in our own broad Doric and they said they loved the sound of it, even though they couldn't understand a word we were saying.

In late afternoon the rain ceased and the vale of Grasmere steamed like a witches' brew. The outline of the lake came gradually into view, the shape of the mountains was revealed, veiled in ghostly mists that hovered on their brows and mingled with the rising clouds. On our first day at Grasmere we saw a search party go by and a helicopter overhead, and yesterday we were told that a climber had been found dead on the shoulder of Silver Howe, which even now was only half visible in the lingering mist.

After supper we locked the tent and motored down to Rydal. There still remained about 26 camps on the squelchy slopes of Dale End Farm, with cars coming and going most of the day between the village and the site. Sometimes the cars had to be pushed out of the mire, but being on the slope I never had any trouble with the Viva.

We walked round the lovely chapel of St. Mary's at Rydal and across Dora's Field to read Wordsworth's verse on a brass plate embedded in a huge rock high up among the stately trees on Rydal Mount. Seen in the spring Dora's Field is a blaze of daffodils and crocuses, said to have been planted by Wordsworth to commemorate the death of his daughter, then Mrs. Edward Quillinan, in 1847. We descended the hill, almost every step a new vista of lake and sky and mountain, and some quaint cottage or manor peeping from the greenery of wood and tree.

On asking the whereabouts of Wordsworth's residence I was directed to a privately owned house on a bend of the road well up the hill. It was a yellow rambling structure with round stone chimneys and high garden walls, so that little more than the roofs were visible, and even these were screened by trees. I would have pried further but the yapping of dogs deterred me, and Jane kept crying me back, so we walked down to Pelter Bridge to watch the torrent on the Rothay Burn after the heavy rains.

Above us on the left was Rydal Hall, where Queen Wilhelmina of Holland stayed with her family in the summer of 1923, and which is now a youth hostel, or something of the sort.

At Nab Cottage I made enquiries of the Coleridges from the landlady. But she could tell me little more than I already knew, except to remind me that De Quincey the opium addict also lived here, before he moved to Dove Cottage, but that there was nothing to be seen in evidence of his tenancy, not a thing. So I thanked the lady politely and went to join Jane on the road again.

69

It was getting dark when we returned to Grasmere. We were surprised and delighted to find the trinket shops alight and still open and the cafe serving snacks on a lighted balcony over the river. I swung into the side and stopped the car to buy some books, for I was hungry to read something of Wordsworth in this lovely country. I managed to find a paper-back of Wordsworth's Poems in The Laurel Poetry Series for 3/6d., which was quite enough for holiday reading, and that I could enjoy them in the location of their composition was a very special thrill. Jane fancied and bought a jug inscribed with a verse and a bunch of Wordsworth's daffodils. Grasmere church was in darkness as we motored through the village and round the silent lake and up the narrow road over the hill and down the dell to the camping site, where most of the tents were alight with bright colours from within; some green, some yellow, some blue, and voices coming from within in a cheery hub-bub, while the lake listened in an eerie stillness.

This was to be our sixth night under canvas and our last in Lakeland. Because of the rain there was much that we had missed; in spite of it much that we had seen. Our chief mission in this Poet's Paradise had been fulfilled, but there were still many shrines in Lakeland we had not visited: places where the poets had touched and sanctified with their presence, writers such as Harriet Martineau, Mrs. Hemans, Charlotte Brontë, Mrs. Gaskell and Matthew Arnold, Samuel Taylor Coleridge, and John Peel in his grave at Caldbeck. Peel and his huntsmen are still very much a tradition of Lakeland, where the hounds and mounted red-coats still give chase to the wily fox. The song was written by John Woodcock Graves. Perhaps we shall come again to this delightful wonderland, and next time we may be blessed with better weather.

August 15th, Tuesday

I slept badly but we rose at 4.30 a.m. to breakfast and to pack our tent and bedding while it was still dry. Only one other camper was astir, obviously for the same reason, to get away from the rain while the roads were still quiet. All the camps were silent, their occupants asleep, while here and there a Herdwick sheep nibbled at the wet grass around them.

Dorothy Wordsworth says in her Journal that there were sheep on the island in her day, though there are no sign of them now. The sky was still overcast and threatening, but daylight was beginning to shape the hills and the lake and the trees, and some flighty starlings flittered down to gather crumbs at the tent doors.

We were on the road by 7 o'clock towards Ambleside, with scarcely any traffic on the roads. We motored through the fearsome Kirkstone Pass, climbing into the mist on the mountain tops, which made us feel as if we were up in the clouds, while the fog blankets swirled away under us into the valleys. Wordsworth used to come this way on horseback, on his way to Penrith, I think to see Mary Hutchinson, who later became his wife, while Dorothy moped for him at home in Grasmere. I drove along fearful ledges with awesome depths on my side while Jane held on to my knee almost in terror, until by and by we reached the summit and Two Brothers Lake came into view in the distance. We glided away down into the quiet valley and eventually reached the shores of lovely Ullswater, where the light tipped waves were almost lapping the road. All was still quiet and pleasure steamers heaving gently at the deserted piers. And thus on to Penrith and Carlisle on the A6 North. The distance from Grasmere to Foveran in Aberdeenshire by this route is 298 miles and it took me ten hours at the wheel (not counting breaks for meals) to cover it. Altogether, in our Lakeland holiday, we drove 744 miles on 17 gallons of petrol at a cost of £4. 15/-. Counting repair to silencer, one pint of oil, and provisions, we spent just over £16, and I think it was one of the most wonderful holidays we have ever enjoyed. I kept myself awake at the wheel with tea and cigarettes (which I know is wrong) and I was "fagged" out by the time we reached Aikenshill. But I wouldn't have missed a moment of it; it was all so very much worth while.

August 16th, Wednesday

One thing I dislike about buying postcards on holiday is that one must post most of them away to friends. This is becoming a fad, equal to the tyranny of the Christmas card, and it seems the only valid reason why you should send a postcard is because the recipient sent you one last year, or because you were rash enough to send one the year before and he or she sent you one back last year. It's a vicious circle that gets wider with the years as friends and relatives increase, and unless you draw the line somewhere the expense is going to get out of hand.

The average postcard nowadays costs about fivepence to sevenpence, postage fourpence and if you send a dozen or 20 cards to your nearest relatives or closest friends it's going to cost you a packet, especially if you are unfortunate enough to be a member of a large family, or have a lot of close friends, or both. This was bad enough at Christmas and the New Year, but now that the habit has embraced the holiday season you are burning the festive candle at both ends, and indeed all the time, because the tyranny doesn't even end with Christmas cards or postcards, but has been extended to herald every family event of the year, and cards for every purpose are on hand for every occasion: Get Well cards for someone admitted to hospital, even though you had been in seeing the patient the day before, when you saw someone else's card, then he saw yours, until the thing becomes a competition and the ward like an art gallery; every sympathiser afraid to be left out of the exhibition, in case he be considered mean or neglectful, or unable to keep up with the Joneses, and every time you go to hospital you spend more time looking at the selection of cards than you do with the patient, just to make sure that every member of the family has been represented, and that yours is included in the array. This whole thing is becoming ridiculous and hypocritical, as if a relative in hospital were but an excuse to have your name in the surgical art galleries, instead of a genuine desire to see the patient well again. And you must post the card, otherwise it would be criminal.

Then we have congratulatory cards for the birth of another member of the ever-widening family circle, who in his or her time will be entitled to a birthday card perennially, besides the hereditary Christmas card and the holiday postcard; and so it goes on, from the cradle to the grave, anniversaries included, matrimonial or condolency, wedding invitations, greetings cards, sympathy cards, retirement cards, thank-you cards or what have you, and the occasional card has become a shower, including the Valentines and the inevitable "rub" or comic postcard from the turnstile at the beach.

As far as Christmas cards are concerned some families have taken refuge in putting a little notice in the local paper that they won't be sending any this year, or ever again, which may be to spite the Post Office rather than to deny their friends a Christmas Greeting, and with the rising cost of stamps who could blame them? But if the postcard fashion gets much further out of hand the same intimation will have to be made at holiday time.

Mind you its a great boost for the stationer, the designers, the publishers, the Post-Office, and nowadays even charities and institutions who make Christmas cards, but unless we put a foot down somewhere—where is it all going to end?

And what I grudge most about the postcard business is that the card you sent to a friend or relative is the one you wanted to keep for your collection, something in your album you could look forward to looking at in your old age, to remind you of past joys, instead of seeing it now on your friend's mantelshelf. Of course the remedy would be to buy two postcards of the same view, one for your friend and one for your album, but surely that is piling on the agony, and though I am no Scrooge I draw the line at this—and by the way it is almost a hundred years since the original postcard first appeared, round about 1874, and Francis Kilvert mentions it in his diary.

August 23rd, Wednesday

Today I visited Mr. Peter Strachan, editor of the Buchan Observer, Peterhead, and he informed me that my last two contributions had been printed in The Fraserburgh Herald. This was a pleasant surprise and he gave me three copies of my essay on Peter Still, which covered three issues of the paper, nine copies altogether, and he promised to see that I got paid for my efforts. He was just leaving the office for lunch when we called (Jane in the car) and I drove him to the foot of Hope Street where he resides with his married sister. We then went to Jane's sister in Gordon Terrace, Betty and her two daughters, Anne and Rhonda, and little Robert, and Grandfather Willox (Jane's father) who resides there. I went back to the Observer

Office in the afternoon, to see the presses at work, which are new, and of the very latest design, and the proprietor, Mr. Scrogie himself took me over the plant, after which I examined some old copies of the newspaper in the files department. There was an elderly woman and a pretty young girl sitting with me at a long wooden table, seated on high stools like dunces at school, them working at something for the newspaper while I turned over the yellowing pages of bygone days, looking for the dates on which I had seen certain films at the local cinemas in my boyhood, old silent movies which have become synonymous with my childhood through the years. Thus I know that on Saturday, February 9th, 1926, at the old Palace in Hanover Street I saw my very first "western", namely Pat O'Malley and Dorothy Mackaill in THE MINE WITH THE IRON DOOR, with Mitchell Lewis, Creighton Hale, Bert Woodruff and Mary Carr, and that on June 8th of the same year I beheld one of the greatest thrills of my boyhood, when mother gave me twopence for the Saturday afternoon matinee to see Richard Talmadge and Eva Novak in LAUGHING AT DANGER, also at the Palace, and on November 2nd, Saturday at "The Picture House" I saw the Dempsey-Tunney Championship Fight, when Tunney claimed the World Heavyweight Title, and the Big Film was THE SECRET KINGDOM, starring Matheson Lang, and the Song Cartoon "Love's Old Sweet Song", when a white ball used to dance along the lyrics on the silent screen while we sang the words in tune. But such things belong to the past, so I bundled up the old files and put them on the shelf again and turned my thoughts to the present. When I arrived back for tea with the others Betty said that my visits to her were but an excuse to go to the newspaper office, and for all the time I spent in the house I suppose I couldn't really deny it. But she forgave me just the same, for most of my relatives know by now that I'm a queer fish, though not the worst for all that.

August 25th, Friday

Jane and I go to Dufftown, where we visited the ruined castles of Balvenie and Auchindoun. We walked over a mile from the car to look at Auchindoun, up a steep cart track and across a field from a deserted farm, wild desolate country and

74

we looked in the old farmhouse but nobody in sight. Sheep everywhere nibbling grass among the rushes and stray cattle lolling about in the sun. The heat was oppressive and forced us to rest several times on the way, and a man who was following us with a camera turned back within sight of the castle. We waited till he came up and took a photograph of the castle in the near distance, explaining that he was English and wanted a photograph of every Scottish castle he could find. He said he filmed them as transparencies and showed them to his family and friends at home and I complimented him on an excellent hobby and he said he didn't mind the expense. Auchindoun was another one for his collection but he said he would have to content himself with a long-shot as he just couldn't go any further in this oppressive heat, while he wiped the inside band of his hat with a handkerchief. I directed him to Glenbuchat and Kildrummy and several others but he said he had already missed a great many castles in the north and would have to come again to photograph more of them. So the man turned back while Jane and I went on over the gorse towards Auchindoun, wild and picturesque on a green knoll overlooking the rolling hills of the Cabrach and circled by the Fiddich burn in the valley. But such an impressive ruin at close quarters, inspiring thoughts of romance and mystery and an introspection of the historical past, wondering what great or terrible things had happened here; what suffering, what joy had these grim walls been witness to?

> Licht was the mirk hour
> At the day dawnin'
> For Auchindoun was in a lowe
> Ere the cock-crawin'.

As the old ballad tells us when Willie Mackintosh, Chief of the Chattan Clan set fire to the stronghold of "Edom o' Gordon" in the sixteenth century, because "Auchindoun" had fought for Mary Queen of Scots. Sheep lay on the hot sunny stones around the castle, and a young couple strolled among the ruins, hand in hand, the youth helping the girl down from the highest places. The boy had long hair and the girl wore trousers, so that it was difficult to know which was which, except that the youth was taller and the girl prettier, with sky-filled eyes and teeth of pearl and her soft brown hair blowing gently across her young sweet face. What dreams were there in this wild place? What joy? What hidden sadness in the smile as she looked up at the youth holding her hand in the ruins of Auchindoun? They brought life back to the ruins as they leaped over the stones and skipped up the steps while Jane and I watched them at our ease, too fagged out with the heat but to stand and gaze.

Pre-historic earth-works encircle the castle and the central tower was built by Cochran, master-mason and ill-starred favourite of King James III. But here the Ministry of Works are at hand with cement and trowel preserving what is left of grim Auchindoun.

It was a long walk back to the car, and then to Balvenie, just outside Dufftown and above the old railway line, now in its death throes. Balvenie gentle and tame in its green lawns compared with Auchindoun, but a great sprawling ruin with its kitchens and great stone ovens almost intact from the past. I gave the guide a two-shilling tip and he took us everywhere and showed us everything and even convoyed us to the gate when parting, while others going in waited their turn. But he explained to us that this was only part of his job and that he had all the grass to cut between times, even the dry moat that surrounds the castle, and rake up the leaves in the autumn, and that when there were a lot of visitors the grass got above him, some days worse than others; but he liked the visitors all the same and agreed that his living depended on them. So at long last I have seen Balvenie and Auchindoun, both of which I have long admired from a distance, especially Auchindoun in its bold setting above the Cabrach, like a giant's armchair on a rising knoll, as seen from a point on the road between Huntly and Dufftown.

We now took the mountain road from Dufftown to Tomintoul, of which my pen-name is a corruption, descending on Cock Bridge and Corgarff, "Over the Lecht Road", as they say in these parts, where the scenery is superb sweeping down from Tomintoul, the whole countryside opening out before you in splendid panorama, the snow-streaked mountains shouldering the background, with long poles by the sides of the road, to guide the snowploughs in winter.

Before we reached Tomintoul however we stopped for tea at

an old lonely house which had once been a grocer's shop, the windows now boarded up and the wooden sign-board above the door now almost unreadable. Here my thoughts of conjecture were aroused and we got out of the car and wandered round the old house and long-forgotten garden, where I came upon a tall yellow flower like ragwort with a very pleasant smell, a sweet mustiness full of the past and its memories, and I smelled it and loved it until I had to pull part of it out to take home. It wasn't a pretty flower by any means, but it filled the car with this gracious fragrance, peopling my thoughts with the families who had once lived here and enjoyed its perfume, and I just couldn't lay it aside. But alas it never grew in our garden, just shrivelled up and died in the rigours of our coastal winter. Jane didn't care for it and I supposed it had no feminine appeal; no visual beauty, but for me that heavenly smell was irresistible.

It was cooler in the evening as we motored down to Cock Bridge, then over the moors to Ballater, then home by Deeside and Aberdeen.

September 6th, Wednesday

Driving home baled straw from Auchmacoy Home Farm, from Denhead Croft precisely, which is on the estate and worked with their equipment. The foreman went there first with the other tractorman, a cart apiece, he with the bale-sledge on the flat leaf, as I had only an old-fashioned box-cart with a harvest frame. This is the first time I have been on these busy roads with a tractor and a top-heavy load of baled straw, a highly responsible job and I am rather proud to be entrusted with it. But of course I have an All-Groups driving licence and my experience as a car driver has given me confidence. All the same I never thought to see the day when I should join the tractor brigade; not at my age, and having spent most of my working life feeding cattle and doing odd jobs, like fencing and stack-building and pulling turnips; but here I am at last, King of the Road and flying on as if I had done it all my life. But the truth is that I had to go on a tractor or eventually find myself out of a job, for such is life on the farms nowadays that unless you can drive something on wheels you are either on the shelf or you have to accept the most menial of jobs. This driving sense has sharpened the wits of the farm worker and improved his image in the social scene; he is no longer the butt of the townsman's jokes but is accepted as a highly intelligent individual who is well capable of taking care of himself in a modern industrialised community.

The Buchans of Auchmacoy are one of the oldest families in Scotland still living on their original estates and still working the lands of their ancestors. Moreso in the case of the Buchan family, for they are taking over more and more farms from their tenants when a lease expires or when an heirless tenant dies or moves out; they have even been known to provide a tenant with financial assistance to vacate a certain farm on their estates they wished to acquire for their own use, and in this they have been encouraged by the Government's "Golden Handshake" to small farmers in favour of amalgamation in land ownership. A lot of people deplore the disappearance of the small holding and blame it for depopulation of the country-side. This may be partly true but it is also a commercial fact that small farms nowadays are unprofitable. The crofts of our forefathers have been on the way out for a decade and the drift to the towns has become almost a necessity. Modern mechanised farming is only practicable on the bigger scale; the factory farm, where there is space for manoeuvre and flexibility and higher returns on output, and the workers on these estates are better off than they would be striving to make a living on one of the crofts that now comprises one of the fields worked by his employer. Indeed I see no future nowadays for the Little Man in agriculture, and the syndicates are gobbling them up as the supermarkets are swallowing the small shop-keepers. Members of some of the family farms will argue that they are doing fine, and so they may be where they are managing without outside labour, but they have to work longer hours for lower wages than the average farmworker, and contract for work on neighbouring farms to keep going. Theirs is a life of sacrifice and dedication which isn't shared by the average worker in agriculture.

Perhaps the Buchans of Auchmacoy stand for one of the better examples of collective farming, for they are really progressive tillers of the soil, using only the very latest equipment and they lack nothing in the way of modern implements and farm machinery. This year they have 700 acres of cereal crop, mostly barley, handled by three combines, with a massive drying kiln and ample storage space. Much of their straw has already been cleared, sold in the swath, and the ploughing-in of next year's wheat crop is already in progress. About a hundred acres of potatoes are also handled and outlying steadings are being converted for winter storage. When a crofter moves out they put a worker in his house and the holdings are in excellent repair, all the renovation carried out by staff masons and joiners from the Home Farm; no ruins or delapidation here on deserted crofts, but everything modern and progressive.

Auchmacoy House faces south from an eminence overlooking a green basin and surrounded by trees and high walls. The best view of the mansion is obtained from the road near the front entrance, which is private: a white baronial structure with high stone chimneys in the Georgian style, three storeyed with bay windows. Auchmacoy and Logie-Buchan are real beauty spots, and what with its green woods and white cottages there is something here to remind me of the English Lake District. The Ythan estuary at full tide has the appearance of an extensive lake, even as far inland as the Sleeks of Tarty, which can be viewed from the old Bridge at Logie, where the road crosses the river to climb the brae to the quaint old church on the hill. But today I was stacking bales on the Braes of Atrochie, like blocks of gold in the autumn sunlight, while the bees hummed in the flowery hedges and the cushats coo-ed in the pinewoods. I could see as far as Benachie and Oxen Craig, and the blue shoulder of Tap o' Noth on the far horizon to the south-east, and to the north I looked over the red loam of Slains and the green knolls of Pitlurg, the autumn countryside mapped out in green pastures and yellow harvest fields. To the east I had the lighter shades of green and gold in the distant sand dunes heaved high on the coast, where the deeper blue of the ocean diffused with the hazy skyline; to the south the straggling village of Newburgh, and the bridge at the water mouth, where the sun glint dazzled the water; the old castle of Knockhall upon the hill, gaunt and lonely in its isolation, and all around me the random farmsteads with their clusters of trees, and people at work in the harvest fields, some with binders and some with combines, according to their different stages of mechanised progress, for there was a lot to be seen and learned while I stacked the straw bales on the sunny braes of Atrochie.

September 10th, Sunday

My wife's fifty-first birthday in the thirty-second year of our marriage. Comes a gorgeous flaming bunch of gold and bronze chrysanthemums from Lorna, wild orchids from Eric in Malaysia, and a frilled underskirt from Beryl and four greetings cards. Oh yes, and £1 from Graham. What I gave Jane is nobody's business, but she deserves it all as a dutiful mother and a devoted, faithful and loving wife. May God bless her and grant us many more years together as pleasant and beautiful as they have been in the past.

September 12th, Tuesday

We drove down to Auchmacoy for two more loads of baled barley straw. My companion tractor-driver had the new (second-hand) long-cart, which arrived yesterday, and he managed to lift around 190 bales to my 100 on the old harvest cart with a frame. These new flat-leaf carts are more a lorry than a cart; lower, longer and more easily loaded and take bigger loads for long-distance haulage, besides saving money on having to pay a contractor to do it with motor lorries.

The loose straw at present costs about £1. 10/- an acre, but may rise to £2 by next year, depending on the demand, and of course the buyer bales it himself, which means a saving of labour and a quicker clearing of stubble for the seller, whereby he gets a flying start with next year's ploughing. But I've heard it said that it isn't the man who is selling the straw that benefits, but the man who is buying it; because he is husbanding cattle and making dung with the straw, which goes back on his land, while the seller, or the grower of cereals is putting nothing back but artificial fertilisers, depleting his land of humus for the benefit of others, and over a period of years may begin to deplete his crops. And there is usually something to be said for what you hear in the countryside; some wisdom in the observation of others, no matter how clever you believe yourself to be. But we have the cattle and we need the straw and we can manage with a minimum of fertiliser. Indeed we have so many cattle that we seldom ever manage to grow sufficient straw to tide us over the winter, and when we have been lavish with fertiliser it merely flattened our crops.

In the first years of the combine-harvesters farmers burned their straw where it lay in the swath. Almost any evening you could see the sky aglow with their fires, getting rid of the stuff quickly and cheaply; all they wanted was the barley, and to hell with the straw, so they set fire to it. There have been experiments with a species of barley that grew a minimum of stalk, particularly with a Swedish variety, which may have been a good thing against lodging the crop, but did nothing to stock the fodder barns for our arctic winters. But all this has changed, and although there may yet be some who burn the shorter stalk there are as many more who can now make good use of it, and far from being a useless commodity the straw is now in great demand, especially in bedding cattle in the great new self-feed courts that are springing up on the farms all over the countryside, replacing the old byres where beasts were tied by the neck and men were enslaved looking after them, an outdated method which has become far too expensive with commercial cattle in the present wages spiral and scarcity of labour, though it may still be favoured with animals for the show rings.

We left Aikenshill at 12 noon and returned with our loads at 6 p.m., which meant 1½ hours on overtime. Our pay has been increased this week by 14 shillings, and a little more for overtime. Average cash weekly wage, after all deductions and without overtime now amounts to £10. 13. 7., besides considerable perquisites.

September 19th, Tuesday

Jane and I to the cinema, the first time in three months, to the Grand Central in Aberdeen's George Street, one of my favourite dream houses, and there I spend seven shillings of my overtime money for two seats on the balcony, where we have never been before, but very few people there. Main feature an X-certificate spook in startling colours and brilliant photography; haunted old mill, cobwebs, chained maniac and bloodstains. THE SHUTTERED ROOM was made at Twickenham by the Troy-Schenck combination and starred the lovely Carol Lynley, with Gig Young, Oliver Reed and Flora Robson in support. Jane thought it only so-so but I think it had real cinema atmosphere and I found it a convincing seat-gripper. Jane never cared much for the cinema anyway, unless it were a woman's weepie like BACK STREET, REBECCA, HOW GREEN WAS MY VALLEY, JANE EYRE or BRIEF ENCOUNTER, and she just hates westerns and gangster movies. In this case the second feature was supposed to be modern cinema for the teenagers but I found it too slick and confusing, the sort of thing that keeps me away. The camera work is too fast and even I cannot follow it. A silly story and trifling incident, YOU'RE A BIG BOY Now featured Elizabeth Hartman, Peter Kastner and Geraldine Paige. And so God Save the Queen.

We are to have breathalyser tests for drivers suspected of being the worse of drink—this from October. But they are not likely to catch me in that sort of state. (Actually they DID catch me, in 1972, when I had indulged myself in two double whiskies and a glass of brandy in a friend's house. I wasn't drunk, but with my mind preoccupied with the events of the evening I went through traffic lights at amber and collided with another car. But the blow-bag didn't change colour so I was let off with a £10 fine for careless driving and had my licence endorsed. No one was hurt and our cars were repaired.)

1968

July 26th, Friday

We are just returned, Jane and I, from a motoring tour of Caithness and Sutherland, covering a distance of some 687 miles in five days, consuming 19 gallons of petrol at a cost of £5 and 13 shillings. We were under canvas for four nights; at Brora, Thurso and Invershin, and we enjoyed every minute, especially at this last site, where we stayed two nights in a field belonging to Mr. Victor Mackay, farmer at Invershin. Here was everything that my poor heart most enjoys: romantic scenery, a battlefield, a fairy-tale castle perched on a crag, the glistening waters of the Kyle of Sutherland, and a railway clinging to the pine-clad mountainsides. The sun was blistering hot and our car like a baker's oven, so that when we left it for a while we could scarcely sit on the upholstery on our return. But the sunny skies gave a warmth and colour to the scenery that is only matched in dreams and wildest fantasies. And oh how lovely and wonderful was Carbisdale Castle; its marble statues and life-like paintings, its guilded halls and fretted staircases, its rich tapestries and stained floors, where we were allowed to wander at will and gaze from the graceful windows on matchless vistas of river wood and hill. Such scenes as these enrich the mind and lift us momentarily from the monotony of our ordinary lives, and with health and peace of mind we are doubly able to enjoy them. We stood upon the ground where the Duke of Montrose fought and lost his last battle, the Battle of Carbisdale (1650), and we looked across the Kyle where the Duke (Marquis) and one of his lieutenants swam to safety, but were later caught on the shores of Loch Assynt, and led south to Edinburgh, where Montrose was executed.

And such beauty we beheld at the Falls of Shin, where we went to watch the salmon leaping on the linn. Indeed I believe that had I enjoyed this environment in my youth I should never have been such an addict of the cinema. Such colour and grandeur charms the eye of the poet that is in me, when I am conscious of a living glow, swept by a sense of ecstasy that ordinary mortals seldom feel, and though I may seem

D   83

vain and egotistic in admitting it, I assure you I am not.

It is ironical that a castle so charming and beautiful as Carbisdale should have been built out of spite by a Countess of Sutherland who had fallen out with her family, so that she could look down her nose with contempt on her relatives as they passed on the railway below, except that she never lived to exercise her scorn, but died before the castle was completed. And although the castle has been stripped of its armoury and period furnishings what remains is powerful evidence of the taste and high ambition of a spiteful woman. Carbisdale is now a youth hostel and its rooms have been thrown open to the members of that society. For five shillings a holiday vagrant can sleep a night in the communal dormitories, sharing cookery at little more expense, which I think is an excellent idea in preserving the structure, and since the resident warden ensures the strictest disciplinary behaviour and routine, little harm can come to the place. But common people now live like lords in mansions where 25 years ago they wouldn't have dared set foot.

Other castles we visited were Dunrobin and Dunbeath, two magnificent structures perched on the cliff-tops, but we had little more than time to take a picture and be off again. Dunrobin is now a school for the sons of gentle-folks (as Jimmy Edwards would say in the television series "Whacko"), and Dunbeath has been purchased by an American shipping magnate for around £83,000. We were just in time to see this middle-aged American and his sons return from a shoot, a liberal-minded man with a breezy, free-for-all nature, and he sent one of his sons to ask if he could help me in any way with information. But I was in a hurry to be off, and so declined his offer; merely stating that I had a historical interest in architecture and wanted to take a picture, which was granted immediately. The castle was not open to the public and I didn't want to become involved with a private family, nor pry into their living quarters, otherwise at a word I do believe Jane and I would have enjoyed the freedom of the house.

This American calls himself St. Clair, which he claims is derived from Sinclair, and that his ancestors were driven from the Dunbeath estates in the Highland Clearances, when they emigrated to America, and from whence he has now returned to purchase the stronghold of the oppressors of his family clan,

84

returning to sunny California periodically to attend to his various enterprises, while workmen here give his castle a complete overhaul, with scaffolding clinging to the ramparts high above the precipice and the blue surging waters of the North Sea. To live in a place so near the cliff-edge would frighten me to death, never mind owning it; yet this American seems happy with his purchase, never giving weather or erosion a thought, that it might eat away the cliff from under his edifice.

We looked at several other castles through our glasses, mostly in ruins, clinging to the cliff-tops like a bat on a wall— Keiss Castle, Old Man of Wick, Girnigoe and Sinclair, Buchollie and Thurso castles—and a tamer glimpse of the Castle of Mey, holiday home of the Queen Mother, purchased in 1952. We also walked round and peeped into the ancient, white-washed kirk of Canisby, with its lichen-green roof, worshipping place of the Queen Mother while in residence at Mey.

On the whole we thoroughly enjoyed our run from Inverness to Wick, the first time we have gone as far as John O' Groats. We have been on this road before, however, as far as Bonar Bridge, and on one occasion, with the A30 Austin van we slept in two laybys, one just north of Inverness, where a garage proprietor threatened us with eviction at bedtime, because he said we were tresspassing on his property, a piece of waste ground adjoining his garage, where he intended further development. After talking to us for a little while however he relented and allowed us to stay, even without charge, sleeping in the van, provided we didn't leave litter, as he didn't want to encourage more trippers on to the site.

The other layby was merely a field gate, where once a croft had stood, within sight of Tain, and for a time I was in some apprehension of the farmer from the nearby steading coming to move us on. But he never troubled us and we were awakened the following morning by the barking of a friendly dog chasing after the tractors in the silage field when the men started work. This is something we just wouldn't risk nowadays because of reported molestation from vandals, but in the early days of our travels we were so keen to get about on slender means that we dared anything in search of new discoveries. We even paid a garage attendant in Midlothian half-a-crown to let us sleep in the rear of our car in his backyard. We didn't have to pay in advance, and he wasn't up when we left in the morning, but like the honest fool I was I dropped the half-crown into his letter-box. Passing these places nowadays, when we recognise them, we are surprised at our own audacity and the risks we took, like the time we camped on the summit of Drumnadrochit, in an old quarry, the only vacant space, as so many others were at the same game, with a car in every available recess, and we couldn't sleep for the rutting of stags in Glen Urquhart. Next morning I missed a gear changing down on Drumnadrochit and free-wheeled a great part of the hill, the car gathering speed and my brakes nearly on fire, until I slurred to a halt on the road verge and engaged second gear, emerging on Loch Ness and Castle Urquhart greatly relieved, and expecting to see the monster.

On that northerly excursion we had branched off to our left on the A837 from Bonar Bridge, via Oykel Bridge and Elphin, within sight of those singularly remote peaks of Suilven and Canisp, en route for Ullapool, down the shores of Loch Broom, to the terrifying aspect of the Corrieshalloch Gorge and the Falls of Measach. On that occasion, because Jane doesn't like ferries and ferryboats I struck inland again to avoid them, to Garve and Strathpeffer, Muir of Ord and Beauly, and thus down by Drumnadrochit as already related.

Our goal was Oban and MacCaig's Folly, so we journeyed down the shores of Loch Ness, calling at Fort Augustus, Spean Bridge and Fort William, breaking our journey for a drive to Glenfinnan, then south to Glencoe. There was no bridge at Ballachulish in those days, and being confronted with a ferry I was obliged to motor round the shores of Loch Leven, just at the time when workmen were realigning the road, the old road still lurching towards the ravine, where the scenery was spectacular, and going south I had the left side furthest from the edge of the cliffs, where I could afford the occasional glimpse at the passing beauties of the loch.

Emerging from Kinlochleven at Laroch I should have held straight on down the shores of Loch Linnhe, on the A828 as a short-cut to Oban, but fearing another ferry on Loch Etive I struck inland again on a long diversion on the A82 over

86

Rannoch Moor and down the Black Mount to Bridge of Orchy, Tyndrum and Dalmally, avoiding Glen Orchy because of the narrow road, and thus through the Pass of Brander to Connel Bridge, where we had to wait in a queue of cars for a train before the bridge was opened, since it served both purposes, road and rail.

The roads were so poorly signposted in those days I consider that I didn't do too badly on this roundabout mystery tour, besides indulging ourselves in some gorgeous scenery we would otherwise have missed.

Once over Connel Bridge our first sight of Dunstaffnage Castle on its lonely rock in Oban Bay was even more rewarding than MacCaig's Folly, which we had come specially to see. MacCaig's Folly is a most uncommon spectacle, like something from the Isles of Greece, the Acropolis and Parthenon of Oban, this roofless Coliseum transplanted from ancient Rome. We stood inside and gazed through the sashless windows into Oban harbour, where it seemed I could stretch out my arm and steal a toy yacht, or a locomotive from the railway station, but for the frowning peaks of Mull across the Firth of Lorn, which dispelled my Gulliverian perception.

On another trip north we did Glen Affric, then circled the Black Isle from Muir of Ord, returning to Conon Bridge, and thus to Dingwall and Evanton, Invergordon and Ballchraggan, from which we made a detour to Portmahomack, with its two novel churches and vast military shooting range, almost to Tarbat Ness, where the lighthouse is the second highest in Scotland, with the lonely shell of Ballone Castle on the sands, where the sound of the sea echoes forlornly within its hollow walls.

Across the Dornoch Firth, on the shores of Loch Fleet, I was fascinated by the crumbling ruins of Skelbo Castle, not to be confused with Skibo Castle, near Dornoch Sands, which is a modern residence. Skelbo entranced me because of the legend persisting that the Maid of Norway was brought ashore here after her drowning in the North Sea, during the ill-fated attempt by Sir Patrick Spens to bring her across the brine for King Edward of England, who waited in Dunfermline toun for her safe arrival.

She was the granddaughter of Alexander III of Scotland,

promised at his death in marriage to Edward's son, who became Edward II of England, and had this marriage been consummated it is unlikely Bannockburn would have been fought.

The ruin is little more than a scrabble of stones on a green mound overlooking the bent grass of Fleet, part of it like a human skull with a flattened crown and empty eye sockets staring out to sea in a deathless watch for the King's daughter of Norway, with the words of the King still sighing in her woods, "And thou maun bring her hame".

I left Jane in the car on the sandy bents and waded up through the long grass and nettles surrounding the ancient edifice, until I stood within the ghostly walls, gazing through the empty eye sockets to the open sea, the sound of the surf in my ears, my mind busy with the rescue (alas too late) of the historic maiden, and I could imagine the sailors and the Laird's henchmen carrying her lifeless body up from the shore, her white limbs chilled blue from long exposure, a numbed sadness in her sallow Nordic features, her golden tresses hanging over the side of the makeshift litter on which they carried her to the castle. The weeping and wailing of the household and then a post-haste to Dunfermline. I wasn't dreaming, just trying to imagine how it had been, when a cold wind whistled through the empty eyes of Skelbo, ruffling the grass on her eyebrows, chilling my cheek like the hand of death, filling my eyes with cold tears until I withdrew my gaze. So I walked back to the car, where Jane was getting impatient, but I stayed to take a farewell picture in colour of sad forlorn Skelbo, alone with the secrets of a storied past.

Approaching Invergordon from the south I observed on our left, high on a hill top, what appeared to be a perfect stone circle, with a lintel across the flanking stones, clearly outlined against the sky, almost in the manner of Stonehenge, but after some research I find it is of Indian origin, a replica of the gates of Negapatam, near Madras, a city captured by General Sir Hector Munro of Novar, built at his expense to give work at a time of local distress, something in the nature of MacCaig's Folly at Oban, but less elaborate or artistic. On the crest of Ben Bhraggie I also noticed the huge statue of the First Duke of Sutherland, like a thin finger pointing at the sky and visible for miles on the road. Our biggest disappointment was Granny's Heilan' Hame, commemorated in the famous Scottish song, which I have known for 40 years, as sung by Sandy Macfarlane —and what do we find?—not a thatched sheilan or cottage with Granny at the door, but a posh flourishing hotel with everything commercialised, even to the car park, so we turned around and came away in disgust. It may be in the name of progress but for the student of folk-lore and social tradition it is also disillusionment.

More rewarding at Golspie however was our discovery of the Pictish Broch at Strathsteven, dating from 200 B.C., on the right-hand side of the road going north, overlooking the seashore, where I stopped the car to examine it. The ruin exists barely three feet above the ground, but still sufficient to give one a fair idea of its construction and outer defences, which were more extensive than I expected, spreading underground in chambered caverns for several yards around the base of the tower. The Broch is situated on a commanding position overlooking the beach, and yet I was puzzled to think why the defenders chose to erect their tower in a position so conspicuous to their enemies, presumably the Norsemen, who must have found the sandy beach a most convenient landing place. In this position the Broch seems more a target for siege rather than a tower of refuge for the local inhabitants. The last Danish landings were reported at Embo, several miles to the south, just beyond Loch Fleet.

But you haven't seen the Dornoch Firth until you motor over the Struie Hill, where the firth and the Kyle of Sutherland are stretched out before you in panoramic splendour towards the mountains of Assynt and Ben More, with the giant shoulder of Ben Wyvis on your left, where he has shadowed you all the way from Muir of Ord, affording you a glimpse at intervals behind the screening trees. From Struie we descended on Bonar Bridge, and this time we turned right at the bridge for Dornoch, pausing at Spinningdale to take a picture of the beautiful castle in the vale, hiding in a canopy of weeping birches that almost defied me to get it in focus.

On our present journey, now beyond Golspie, and approaching Dunrobin Castle, a deck-chair fell from the roof-rack of the car in front and I ran over it before I could stop. But the other

89

driver was mostly at fault, for he should have had the thing securely tied, so we both apologised to each other and I drove off, leaving him to straighten out the buckled chair, since our own car had sustained no damage.

We camped for the night at Brora, and next day we passed through lovely Helmsdale, with its crag of a castle overlooking the harbour, where I am told that a wine poisoning in 1567 by the Countess of Caithness inspired the death scene in Shakespeare's HAMLET. Thence to Berriedale with its fine new roadway that has straightened out the steep and dreaded hairpin bends, and beyond this on our left we observed for many miles the innumerable scrabble of ruinous crofts on the barren hillsides, the sickly evidence still extant of the Highland Clearances.

Wick we enjoyed, and which I compared with Ayr and Dumfries, because of the river running through the town, but less lovely than these places, and the once busy harbour now a bit of an eyesore. Here we did some shopping and I had a look at the local cinema display, rather a drab scene nowadays and mostly gone over to bingo. At John O' Groats I walked to the utmost edge of the pier and looked into the deep blue water and across the Pentland Firth to Stroma, the nearest of the Orkney Islands, just to assure myself that I had stood on the most northern tip of Scotland, just as I intended some day to stand on the most southern tip at Burrow Head or the Mull of Galloway. Stroma lies about seven miles from the mainland, and with the binoculars we could pick out the crofts scattered on the island, and even the sheep like tiny white seeds on the moors.

I suppose everybody knows the story of John De Groot, a Dutchman who ran a ferry service to Orkney and charged 4 pence a trip, and the little coin became known as a groat; thus John O' Groats, and you can still see his gravestone some three miles away, in the churchyard at Canisbay. He lived during the reign of James IV (1488-1513) but I'm not sure if anyone knows how old De Groot was when he died.

We pitched camp at Thurso, surrounded by tents and caravans on the sea-shore, and within sight of the castle, with its old cannons pointing out to sea. Next morning while shaving I caught sight of the Old Man of Hoy, about 40 miles away across the water, a stack of black rock clearly discernible near the cliffs on the island. And thus on to Dounreay, where we passed the gates of the Atomic Research Establishment, its great dome white and forbidding in the morning sunlight. But what was more important to me was that this was the neighbourhood and burial ground of Henry Morrison Henderson, the Bard of Reay, whose works I bought at the next stopping place, and which I have since enjoyed immensely, as also with the word music of that other Caithness songster, alas no more, the late Alexander Miller. Bettyhill and Tongue are beautiful, and at one stage of our journey we seemed very near to Ben Loyal, blue and shimmering in my glasses, much richer in verdure than the harsh colourless peaks rising inland to the horizon in almost lunar remoteness.

We stopped at Durness and Jane went into Mr. Mackay's shop for provisions, and where she also bought me a postcard view of Smoo Cave because there wasn't time to explore it. You just can't see everything you want to see on holiday and you've got to draw the line somewhere, seeking out only that which seems most interesting in the circumstances. From Durness we drove down the west coast to Kylesku ferry-crossing, but unfortunately it began to rain and we lost much of the spectacular scenery. The roads here are nerve-wracking, real cliff-hangers, with passing places on the edge of deep ravines and black water which frightened my wife nearly out of her wits. Somewhere on the way a signpost pointed 16 miles to the ferry, and driving in the drizzle and lowering sky I thought it the longest 16 miles I had ever driven. At one point the road narrowed to a mere ridge between two frightening gorges, swept with black mist and driving rain, and for the first time in my driving experience I felt nervous at the wheel. Up to now Jane had the worst of it, but now there were gullies on both sides and I shared some of her uneasiness, bearing in mind that there was no escaping Kylesku, our first ferry crossing.

But at last we drew up behind three other cars waiting for the ferry, and once on board we were soon across, still sitting in the car and staring down at the dark deep water. Once across Kylesku I filled our petrol tank and drove in search of a camping site. The rain had ceased and the sky cleared but we drove mile upon mile without much sign of civilisation. Quite late in the evening we descended upon the shores of Loch Assynt, with the bold outline of Quinag in the background. It was here that the great Montrose was captured by Neil MacLeod and held in Ardvreck Castle until he was led to execution in Edinburgh. But a mere fragment remains of the castle, a gaunt lonely structure across the blue waters from Quinag. We had almost given up hope of finding a communal camping site when lo, we rounded a bend and there was Invershin Farm and a field full of caravans and tents of all colours, a welcome sight indeed, and when we saw the castle above it, fairytale Carbisdale, perched on its crag like a picture from a child's story book—it was almost too much to hope for and our spirits rose with the prospect.

Oh yes Mr. Mackay would take us in, and we could stay as long as we liked, but I said that two days would be sufficient to see the neighbourhood, Carbisdale included. Mr. Mackay was just making his last round of the site before bedtime, after a busy day in the hay field, and being a farm worker myself I assured him I knew how he felt. Next morning by cock-crow our bacon and eggs were spluttering in the frying-pan on the gas stove just outside the tent door, while Jane and I ate a grapefruit between us with teaspoons; it's good for your digestion, besides giving you an appetite. Already the sun was out bright and happy, clapping his joyful hands and urging us to be off for another day of glorious exploration, beginning with Carbisdale; beautiful, captivating Carbisdale, so I got out of the car and took a photograph of the castle through an arch of the railway viaduct, a magnificent framework for a structure of such intrinsic beauty.

At Bonar Bridge I left Jane in the car and was away for an hour, which alarmed her considerably, for lo, I walked into the tourist information centre to ask about Carbisdale, and there I met a most remarkable man; poet, scholar, gentleman and soldier, one-time guide for the exhibition department on electronics at Dounreay Atomic Research Station, and now giving out information for tourists at this gateway to Ross and Cromarty, Sutherland and Caithness. We cracked away for an hour on kindred subjects, exchanging signatures and pet notions, and Mr. William Sinclair of Blandfield, Bonar Bridge, reading aloud to me some of his poems in manuscript. A veteran of both World Wars "Willie" Sinclair does not look like a man well into his seventies; a man with a message in his speech and well qualified to lecture; yet he, like myself had little schooling, being one of a family of 11 children born to a Highland shepherd, and he told me that one of his brothers had later managed to purchase the 400 acre farm on which his father had been employed. Mr. Sinclair has a keen sense of injustice, and he pointed it out to me where I never knew it existed. He gave me a new slant on commerce and compared it with the feuds of the Barons in mediaeval times, except that public money— stocks and shares—are used instead of musket and claymore, and that the Stock Exchange Market has taken the place of the battlefield. He lectured me on history and municipal diplomacy, but in composition he has confined his efforts mainly to letters in the press, which editors have sometimes refused to publish, perhaps because of their vituperation against an evil they had no wish or no reason to expose, perhaps to safeguard their revenue from advertising sources, or simply to save their own skins or reputation against bureaucracy. Our author-poet writes his poetry for his own amusement, perhaps without thought of print or public recognition.

At the end of this entry I will give an example of Willie Sinclair's poetry, but meantime he had detained me long enough, quite unaware, until I told him that Jane was waiting for me in the car, and probably at her wit's end for my safety, not knowing exactly where I had gone, and afraid to leave the car lest I should return in her absence and go looking for HER. So Mr. Sinclair left his office and came with me to apologise to Jane for keeping me so long, shaking hands with her and taking all the blame for my prolonged absence.

Actually, in meeting Willie Sinclair of Bonar Bridge I had inadvertently tracked down the subaltern who prompted Field Marshal Montgomery to ban the wearing of top hats in the Eighth Army. Willie was a Staff Sergeant with the Canadian Seaforths, and for unexplained reasons was attached to the regimental "Intelligence" group—"probably because I was the despair of the drill sergeants". In his own words "I became a sort of Father Confessor and confidante to all ranks; only four of us First War lads went overseas, the remainder were culled, and I was put in charge of the Regimental Post Office". The

93

battalion was stationed at Danny House, just north of Brighton, and Staff Sergeant Sinclair made use of the old wine cellar as a sorting house for the mail. One day he was visited by an old cronie from World War I, namely Dutch Artz, who between the wars had become something of an entertainer, and on this occasion he was laden with about a dozen top-hats, which he intended to use in a charity show he was putting on for the local village children.

Dutch Artz twirled one of the hats on his finger-tip and with a quick flick of the hand he landed it on Willie Sinclair's head. Willie was busy with the outgoing mail, and when Artz left he was so much preoccupied that he forgot all about his new head-gear, and he was still wearing it when the Colonel came in. Remembering the top-hat Willie immediately took it off. "No no, postie", said the Colonel, "leave it on, the boys will get quite a diversion out of it."

Henceforth, to the amusement of all ranks Willie stuck to his top-hat, until he was rebuked by the Regimental Sergeant Major. "Postie", barked the R.S.M., "you of all people, who should be setting an example to the lads. That you should so disgrace yourself and the battalion in this manner. Take it off man!" But Willie explained politely to the R.S.M. that he had the Colonel's permission to wear the hat. "You old rascals are all alike", said the R.S.M., "you are all beyond redemption!"

In 1943 the battalion went overseas to Sicily, where Staff Sergeant Sinclair was still wearing his top-hat. They were encamped on the lower slopes of Mount Etna when he got a wire instructing him to collect mail from the outlying units. It was the day before the Canadian Seaforths were to cross the Straits of Messina for Calabria in Italy, so postie Sinclair set out in a cabless 15 cwt. light lorry, driver provided, when they met Field Marshal Montgomery and his entourage in open cars inspecting the forward positions. Willie says Monty's dress order was cheerfully ignored, and that he continued to wear the top-hat until he lost it around the town of Ortona-mare, where the Seaforths had a very rough time—"and my well-worn, much respected topper went missing!"

In his memoirs, published in 1958, on page 191, Montgomery states: "The men in back areas discarded all possible clothing and some even took to wearing the wide-brimmed Sicilian

94

straw-hat. I well remember an incident that occurred one day I was driving in my open car up to the front. I saw a lorry coming towards me with a soldier apparently completely naked in the driver's seat, wearing a silk top-hat. As the lorry passed me, the driver leant out from his cab and took off his hat to me with a sweeping and gallant gesture. I just roared with laughter. However, while I was not particular about dress so long as the soldiers fought well and we won our battles, I at once decided that there were limits. When I got back to my headquarters I issued the only order I ever issued about dress in the Eighth Army; it read as follows: 'Top hats will not be worn in the Eighth Army'."

Writing to me in 1979, at the "contemptible" age of 83 Willie Sinclair says: "Contrary to the General's tab, I was NOT sitting in the driver's seat, and I WAS wearing my regulation bush shirt and shorts, which apparently had escaped Monty's observation, or perhaps 'apparently completely naked' suited his purpose in highlighting the incident".

Willie Sinclair also sent me the following philosophical lines he copied from a beer mug in a Sussex tea-room while stationed in the Downs in midsummer 1941:

"Let the wealthy and great roll in splendour and state,
I envy them not I declare it.
I eat my own lamb, my own chicken and ham,
I shear my own fleece—and I wear it.
I have lawns, I have bowers, I have fruit, I have flowers,
The lark is my morning alarmer;
So jolly boys now—Here's God speed the plough,
Long life and success to the farmer."

But to continue our journey: After two days of joyous bliss at Invershin and Lairg we came south to Tain, where we went into the very old pewless church of St. Duffus, which I presume is the shrine attributed to St. Duthac, erected in 1471 and visited annually by King James IV in penance for his father, James III. The King made his last pilgrimage in August, 1513, exactly one month before he was killed at Flodden. The stained glass windows in this wondrous chapel are among the most beautiful we have ever seen. It was also at Tain that the first queen of Robert the Bruce, the Lady Margaret of Mar,

95

betrayed by the Lord of Ross, was captured by the English after her flight from Kildrummy Castle in Aberdeenshire.

Returning to Inverness and the Moray Firth we looked in at Fort George, where I was much impressed by the dignified armorial dedication to King George II (1683-1760), a challenge and symbol of regal authority, chiselled in stone above the main entrance and facing the courtyard. It also intrigued me to think that James Boswell had preceded me here by nearly two hundred years. We spent an exhausting but profitable hour at the fort's extensive museum of uniforms, weaponry, paintings, medals and regimental history, where I verified much of what I already knew of the fortress and the reasons for its existence in this sea gateway to the Highlands of Scotland.

THE LASS O' SPINNINGDALE by WILLIE SINCLAIR of "Blandfield" Bonar Bridge, Sutherland.

Oh! welcome happy youthful prime, wi' opening bud and
    blade,
It's fine to hear the birdies sing in every greeny glade;
The burnies running sweet and clear through every lovely
    vale—
They mind me o' my bonnie dear, the Lass o' Spinningdale.

When summer busks the banks and braes, wi' verdure fresh
    and green
And nature in her mantle gay on every hand is seen,
When springing flowers and vocal air each raptured sense
    assail
They mind me o' my bonnie dear, the Lass o' Spinningdale.

To wander where the winding streams play o'er the rocky harp,
When on the tide the morning beams the shadows softly warp,
And muirland choirs wi' music rare the rays o' morning hail—
They mind me o' my bonnie lass, the Lass o' Spinningdale.

To wander out by Crrek Dhu high where lonely rests the
    clouds,
Or through the lovely Fairy Glen amid its bonnie woods,
Or travel Achues many miles where silence reigns supreme—
I must return to Spinningdale, this island of my dreams.

August 19th, Monday

Jane and I are off again for another motoring holiday in joyous Lakeland. But this time we made a different approach, driving down the east coast of Scotland (instead of the west coast) to Berwick-on-Tweed, and to Alnwick, where we branched off into the Northumberland hills towards Rothbury, Hexham and Penrith to Keswick and Cockermouth.

We spent little time in Scotland and made our first crossing of the new Tay Road Bridge and our third of the Forth Road Bridge, paying half-a-crown for each crossing. Thence by Leuchars and St. Andrews and most of the Fife coast villages; Kingsbarns, Crail, Kilrenny, Anstruther, Pittenweem and St. Monance. Here we were prevented from reaching the squat little fourteenth-century church by an ale lorry which blocked the narrow street by the harbour. We waited for nearly 20 minutes and rain drops began to splatter the windscreen, so I backed out and made off for the main road again, observing in my mirror another motorist do likewise, who had been sandwiched between us and the lorry.

Once through Kirkcaldy, Burntisland and Inverkeithing, we crossed the Forth and skirted Edinburgh, passing through Leith to North Berwick and Tantallon on the coast, and thus by delightful Eyemouth (2¼ miles off the main road) to Berwick-on-Tweed. The rain was now heavy (despite the favourable weather forecast, which had decided my choice for this route) and the car was faulty, so we had to arrange for bed-and-breakfast at the house of the proprietors of the Border Garage, Mr. and Mrs. C. Chisam, 126 Castlegate, where we were charged a modest £1 each for comfortable lodgings overlooking the railway station and the Royal Border Bridge. My only complaint was the noisy traffic on the High Street, heavy vehicles passing south and chasing sleep from our pillows.

Next morning I rose early to wash and shave before anyone required the bathroom, and before breakfast I left Jane to dress and went to explore the railway yard and the splendid viaduct which carries the trains over the Tweed. The station occupies the site of Berwick Castle, where the English Parliament ceded the Scottish throne to John Balliol in preference to Robert

Bruce, Earl of Carrick, at the behest of Edward I of England in 1296, 18 years before Bannockburn.

After breakfast, and our car repaired, which cost us 12/6d., plus 2/6d. tip to the mechanic, we pitched our tent on the Stephenson Campus on the links and went to explore the town. Next day (Tuesday, 20th) we walked round the city walls and examined every bastion on the sea and landward sides: Meg's Mount, The Cumberland, Windmill and Brass Bastions, over the Scot Gate and the Elizabethan Arch at Cowport to the King's Mount, along the riverside until we emerged at the parapet of the old Jacobean bridge at the foot of West Street.

Since my days of mud bridges I have been enthralled by the prospect of a walled city, but never till now have I had the opportunity of seeing one—and here was me walking round the walls of Berwick in fulfilment of a childhood dream, and with the probable exception of York I am doubtful if this could be done nowadays with any other city in Britain. And here I couldn't help making comparison with Fort George, for although the fortifications here are much older (sixteenth century) they are remarkably well preserved and impressive in their strength. From the area of Black Watch Tower I could trace the remains of the Edwardian earthworks, probably known as the Ditches, erected during the Wars of Independence to repel the Scots, but these are little more than mounds and trenches which, but for their regular outline, might be mistaken for the works of nature.

We were tempted but hadn't the time or the patience to inspect the Ravensdowne Barracks and Regimental Museum of the King's Own Scottish Borderers, which is the equivalent of what we saw concerning the Queen's Own (Seaforth and Cameron) Highlanders at Fort George, for I do like making comparisons. The entrance to Berwick Barracks is ornamented by the armorial insignia of George I, whereas the coat of arms of George II welcomes (or repels) the visitor to the Moray Firth fortress which bears his name, bearing in mind that George II was brother to "Butcher" Cumberland, whose vile name is perpetuated by a bastion in both forts.

But these excursions are so exhausting in stifling heat so I contented myself with a half-crown booklet on the fortifications of Berwick-upon-Tweed and betook ourselves to the cooler shades of the ancient Parish Church of the Holy Trinity, with its wilderness of long-forgotten gravestones, waist-high grass and fallen trees. This venerated structure was built in 1650-52 with stones from Berwick Castle and it is remarkable that the city ramparts have not been robbed over the centuries for similar purposes, as seems to have happened in Alnwick, where only the main Norman gateways remain. The eventual demolition of Berwick Castle seems to have been inevitable in the pathway of the railway where it crosses the Royal Border viaduct, one of the most remarkable bridges I have ever seen, built by Robert Stephenson in twenty-eight arches on a wide arc across the Tweed estuary and opened in 1850 by a youthful Queen Victoria. A curtain wall is all that remains of the castle, and this I would have liked to view from the river, where its elevation and impregnable strength would be seen to the best advantage.

The Guildhall (1662) dominates the town and the three bridges at Berwick are a lesson on period architecture and social development. We just had time to walk round the picture gallery at the library in Marygate where the stall-holders were setting up their produce for sale when we left the town on Wednesday morning, August 21st, the vendors occupying half of the street and most of the parking space in front of the Guildhall on market days.

On leaving Berwick-on-Tweed, to reach the battlefield of Flodden, I had to leave the coast road and make a detour on the A698 to Coldstream, where we found the fatal field about two miles further south on the A697 to Newcastle, on Branxton Hill, but with no other distinctive features on the right-hand side of the road. Was this the best the Scots King could do by way of strategy?—or did he have no other choice? Certainly his Stuart ancestor of 199 years earlier would have chosen differently—as he did at Bannockburn. Perhaps King James IV was a bit cocksure of himself with such a grand body of men behind him, the flower of Scotland's knighthood.

The Scottish army at Flodden in 1513 numbered merely 26,000 men, yet it was estimated to be the largest, grandest, and finest army ever assembled north of the border. Surely this must be a contradiction of the facts, because in 1314 Bruce led 32,000 pikemen against the English at Bannockburn, the bravest band of heroes ever to stick a spear in an English breast, if we are to trust to Barbour and the history books, and on that occasion the Scots faced the greatest and grandest force of Englishmen ever gathered for civil strife within the British Isles, something like 100,000 men, outnumbering the Scots by nearly three to one, with the best archers and the finest cavalry in Europe. Indeed the Scots at Flodden were numerically superior to their English opponents, but by the end of the day, fighting round their king, they could scarcely keep their feet to strike a blow, slipping in the warm blood of their fallen kinsmen.

King James IV left Edinburgh with his soldiers on August 19th, 1513, and on Friday (Bloody Friday) September 9th, they were massacred on Branxton Hill, near Flodden, a name synonymous with Culloden two centuries later in the shedding of Scottish blood. The Scots at Flodden carried spears 15 feet long, while the English fought with halberds of 8 feet, which they used as axes, hacking the Scots to pieces, encumbered by their unwieldy lances, more suited for cavalry than for foot soldiers. I suppose we have learned most of this from the works of William Dunbar, who was court-poet to King James IV, a monarch who had done more to bring stability and prosperity to Scotland than any other in the preceding two centuries. But alas for James and for Scotland, and despite all advice to restrain him, Flodden was a fatal gamble which bled the Scots of the flower of their younger men for nearly a generation, and avenged the English for Bannockburn. And whereas Edward II escaped from Bannockburn King James died at Flodden, cut down in the last moments of battle, leaving his country at the mercy of his enemies.

His venerable body, encased in lead after the battle, became the sport of taxidermists and antique hunters, and his noble head, which ignored advice at Flodden, was eventually severed and buried among the common merchants at Cheapside, London, without a memorial and since demolished. What surprises me is that the English didn't exploit their victory and take over the Scottish nation, stripped of her manhood and almost defenceless, but such is history.

In the epic poem of MARMION Sir Walter Scott gives us

almost an eye-witness account of the Scottish army marshalling
for Flodden on the southern outskirts of Edinburgh:

A thousand did I say? I ween,
Thousands on thousands there were seen,
That chequered all the heath between
The streamlet and the town;
In crossing ranks extending far,
Forming a camp irregular;

Oft giving way, where still there stood
Some relics of the old oak wood,
That darkly huge did intervene,
And tamed the glaring white with green:
In these extended lines there lay
A martial kingdom's vast array.

From West to East, from South to North,
Scotland sent all her warriors forth.
Marmion might hear the mingled hum
Of myriads up the mountain come;
The horses' tramp, and tingling clank,
Where chiefs review'd their vassal rank,
And charger's shrilling neigh;
And see the shifting lines advance,
While frequent flashed, from shield and lance,
The sun's reflected ray.

They saw, slow rolling on the plain,
Full many a baggage cart and wain,
And dire artillery's clumsy car,
By sluggish oxen tugged to war;
And there were Borthwick's Sisters Seven,
And culverins which France had given.
Ill-omen'd gift! the guns remain
The conqueror's spoil on Flodden plain.

Approaching Alnwick I was greatly impressed by the massive
spectacle of Alnwick Castle with its statues on towers and
turrets, seemingly hurling defiance at marauding Scots who
would venture thus far south, especially after Flodden, which

should have taught the kilted hordes a lesson. But leaving history behind I soon found my thoughts taking a turn for the supernatural, or at least for the bogey of superstition, for on Alnwick's narrow main street, in an olde English casement window, which had once been a vintner's shop, I observed an array of wine bottles which have remained untouched by human hands for 150 years. The corks have rotted to crumbs and the wine has evaporated and dried away from years of sun exposure. A mellowing card in the window informs passers by that a man dropped dead while stacking the bottles and that anyone trying to remove them will share a similar fate.

Five minutes later, on the same street, I was involved in a frustrating traffic jam where two heavy lorries had entangled, their drivers at their wits' end trying to free them. Is it possible that a man with a bulldozer is afraid to demolish the buildings where the bottles are stacked to have the street widened, the main thoroughfare of the town? Or is it just one more of those crafty municipal gimmicks to intrigue the tourist? The cobwebs are an excellent advertisement for the wine vendor (still in business) but provoking to the student of progress. The least that could be done is surely to install lights for the control of single lane traffic, as has been done over the bridge on the northern approach to Alnwick.

I have never been back there and I just wonder if anyone has ever been bold enough to remove the wine bottles—or if they still remain there as a challenge to the timorous, cluttering up the main street in defiance of modernity and shuttling traffic? All the same I will admit I wouldn't be the one to volunteer to shift the wine bottles—I'm far too superstitious for that.

Thus across Northumbria to Rothbury, Hexham and Penrith, via the A686 over Pike Rigg, Black Fell and Hartside Hight, with stupendous descents and kaleidoscopic landscapes in sun-painted colours, alarming for the faint-hearted on the steepest slopes. From Penrith we motored straight to Keswick, where the sun made pastel shades on the bracken; where the hills were mottled with purple heather and white ribbons of water sparkled on the fells.

We had motored right across England and I was tired and irritable when we reached Cockermouth. But quite unknowingly, in search of a parking space we stopped directly opposite Wordsworth's birthplace, and the excitement of seeing the house revived my interest. And such a wealth of lore is here for one like me, for whom the title of a book shines like a beckoning star, buckling me to further discovery in a pilgrimage I may never be able to repeat. I am not a young man with the hopes of a second exploration, for the opportunities of travel have come to me fairly late in life, so I take in all I can with one visit, my mind working with computer activity in memorising all that the eye, nerves and brain can cope with.

After the usual exhibits we were introduced to a grand piano of Wordsworth's period, sadly out of tune because it was built on a wooden frame that had warped, and which gave its makers a lesson which taught them all pianos should henceforth have an iron frame. We were not permitted into the upstairs bedroom where the poet was born, but I was allowed to take a picture of Jane on the terrace at the foot of the garden, where Wordsworth and Dorothy played as children, and which he mentions in The Prelude, with the river Derwent flowing gently behind us.

This to me is a heaven where my soul has already visited, where my physical presence has made it a reality, and in moments like these I appreciate the true meaning of a heaven upon earth, though I may only snatch at it, as if it were a passing butterfly.

Thursday 22nd of August was the day of the Grasmere sports and it was raining. Lakeland lowered from dark eyebrows of heavy rain cloud; scowling where you had looked for smiles, and your garden of yesterday was now become a depressing wilderness. But Lakeland is such a wanton mistress that one peep from the sun is like a candle of hope for drooping spirits. Her face dimples into smiles where ever a sunbeam should light, be it but the merest patch of sun on fern or bracken, the gentlest glint of sun-kissed lake, a wisp of mist festooned on the fells, and your spirit warms with the opening prospect.

This year we were camped at Causeway Foot Farm, owned by Mr. and Mrs. Nicholson, a well organised site with toilets and showers and plugs for electric razors. A room at the farmhouse had been turned into a shop for the sale of groceries, sweets and cigarettes, while milk could be had on the field.

There were fire hoses at the gate and a public 'phone box at the roadside.

Here we stayed for three days and nights enclosed by entrancing hills and dreamy valleys that smiled in different colours at every passing cloud. And such a feast is here for the restful soul that hungers for bliss, and your sun-filled eye goes roaming on the hill-crests for reflected gold, bewitched by every bush and folded tree on nature's rumpled apron, and her breast glances with cameos of priceless beauty.

But I was not interested in the Grasmere Sports, neither of hounds or sprinters on Butter Knott Hill, and anyway, when we reached Grasmere it was pouring rain. We waited till after dinner, when the sky began to clear, and we made off in search of Hard Knott Pass, the highest navigable road in Britain, higher they tell me than Applecross in Scotland. But first we had to tackle Wrynose Pass (how appropriate the names are) the first landing on this mountain staircase. On the summit of Wrynose I stopped the car to have a look back and couldn't get it going again. The car was at such an angle that the petrol pump couldn't bring fuel from the tank at the rear to the carburettor in front. It was a terrifying moment and Jane got in a panic lest I should let the Viva run backwards. A motorcyclist stopped and said that unless our car was in first class fettle we shouldn't try the Hard Knott Pass. We thought that Wrynose was steep enough but he said that Hard Knott was steeper, and could be dangerous if the car stalled. Eventually I got the car going and Donald Broadwell said that if we drove behind him he would lead us to a side road where we could avoid Hard Knott Pass. He gave me his address at 12 Ripley Street, Lightcliffe, near Halifax, Yorks, England, and before he left us I took his picture with Jane standing beside the car. He talked with us for the better part of an hour, sitting astride his machine. Referring to our son being abroad he told us he had served in the Far East against the Communist Guerillas and knew Malaysia well, and he gave us a good description of the country and its people. Eventually he pulled down his goggles from his helmet, put on his gloves, kicked up his bike and was off, waving to us as he went roaring up the Hard Knott Pass, and we watched him until he became a mere speck in the rising distance. Cars were like mites on a cheese, crawling up the spiral track, and we heard the roaring of their engines nearly a mile away. These mountain passes were used by smugglers in the old days and the tank crews were trained on them during the last war.

Next day we went to Coniston, where I promised myself last year I would return to see Brantwood Manor, home of John Ruskin, on the shores of the lake, a view which caught at our very breathing, lifting our gladdened hearts with a hymnal joy. We looked at this scene from Ruskin's lancet windows, cut in stone and known as the Seven Lamps of Architecture, and from his study windows, where the beauty of the scene seemed more of a bewitching distraction rather than an inspiration for the mind of a busy writer. But I suppose it is possible to accustom one's self to festival as to squalor, and work to a purpose in spite of either.

But here I was in this sunlit sanctuary, far from the harvest fields of Aberdeenshire, where I have laboured under the halo of this great man's presence, snatching an essay with every mealtime, never dreaming to be blest with a visit to the well-spring from which my fountain flowed. Can you marvel that I lingered on every relic with miser zeal?—on every sketch and water-colour; on every shell and pebble and scrap of manu-script, on every map drawing of Ruskin's boyhood, at his books all lined with calf and embossed with golden titles, at the list of celebrities he had entertained, every photograph and framed newspaper cutting, going from room to room with a guide-folder in my hand (for want of a human guide) till my wife wearied of waiting, and all the time my mind opening to the genius still breathing at Brantwood. In a painting of Ruskin's mother I was intrigued by a spot of sunlit landscape framed in a window; an inset, or a picture within a picture, done by Richmond or Collingwood, but here memory fails me. It was one of those curios in a painting mostly pointed out by experts but this one I found in the guide book and spotted for myself.

In the afternoon we visited Cartmel Priory, where Mole Richardson technicians were preparing their equipment for a television broadcast, their great arc-lamps concentrated on the architectural features of the interior, but robbing the coloured windows of their transparency. But it is a mighty building of great antiquity and being in England has been spared the desecration of John Knox and the Reformation.

Cartmel is a typical Lakeland village of painted houses, flowering rockeries and spotless shops; a land where hedges are pruned and dykes are rebuilt and where litter is a sin; all contrasting bitterly with a Scotland of slag heaps, scrapyards, rubbish dumps, nettle gardens and ruined houses; where every layby is a bin-yard, and surely here is a comparison that we Scots should be ashamed of, that here at least the English can teach us a lesson in social habits we have yet to learn.

And how clear and sparkling were the waters of Duddon, gemmed with rocks and shining pebbles, fringed with berried rowan and leaning ash, splashing under a hump-back bridge where an old man sat on the parapet. Here we had tea in our deck chairs and lazed in the toasting sun. That I should live to enjoy such luxury rewards the strenuous labour of my arduous youth, and I am indeed thankful to have plucked the grapes which always seemed so unobtainable.

From Broughton we drove to Grange on Sands, overlooking Morecambe Bay, and thus to Newby Bridge and up the side of Windermere Lake to Hawkeshead, where this time we made a point of looking at Ann Tyson's Cottage, white as snow with purple clematis flowers on the walls. And in the Minstrel's Gallery there was a miniature house for Snow White and her Seven Dwarfs (which I believe I mentioned last year) and one for Beatrix Potter's Little People, all so reminiscent of Lakeland and its Fairytale Poets.

On the way home from Lakeland this year we stopped at Ecclefechan to visit the birthplace of Thomas Carlyle. While we were here the custodian from Carlyle's other house in Chelsea, with two woman companions, called at the door, and while our guide entertained them he told us to go upstairs and look around. So I kissed my wife in the room where Carlyle was born, almost at his bedside (but not the original) while Jane Welsh watched us enviously from the wall. I rocked Carlyle's cradle, put on his hat and sat in his chair, for here was I, a very peasant of his day, now enjoying a social freedom he never dreamed of, and earning almost as much from my physical labour as he did from a scholarship, and gallivanting the country in a manner that riches couldn't buy in Carlyle's day.

This year we did 840 miles and the petrol cost us £7. 4/-. We arrived home at Aikenshill at 8.35 in the evening of Saturday, August 24th.

September 1st, Sunday

Today we were in two churches, namely the parish church at Clola and the Episcopal church of St. John at Longside; this latter being a very beautiful building with fine statues and colourful windows and some relics of the Rev. John Skinner, author and poet of the parish in the eighteenth century. The original kirk was burned down by the Redcoats after the '45 rebellion, and the Rev. Skinner preached from the kitchen window in his farmhouse at nearby Linshart, while his congregation gathered round a huge tree in the farmyard, known as the Linshart Tree, which was still standing when I worked on a neighbouring farm, but was blown down in 1953.

We then motored to Stuartfield, some six miles distant, where we met Mrs. Margaret Clark, now in her 79th year, and who has recently made a name for herself locally with her reminiscences, both in prose and poetry in the BUCHAN OBSERVER. She is a shepherd's widow with a wonderful memory and a command of words and the doric which enables her to re-live the past with a zest and nostalgia that others can share and enjoy, and her store of local worthies and village anecdotes are well worth recording. She lives with her family in a new council house, and because we couldn't talk to her privately we took her into the car, where she gave us most of her life story. I gave her my pen-name and she said she had read and enjoyed some of my stories. The editor had never paid for her contributions but had sent her a delightful hamper of provisions and flowers, which perhaps he thought would be more useful at her age.

It was a delightfully sunny evening when we left Stuartfield and we drove up past Crichie House on the road to Toddlehills and Arnage, in the very heart of Buchan, which I now fondly think of as Toulmin Country, since my stories of the area have been published and so widely read. It's not that I mean to be vain mind you, or even egotistic, for I am considered a very modest person; it's just a little glow of satisfaction I feel for putting the land of my birth on the world map, where all may feel its snell winds and the damp of its clinging mists; its driving sleet and frosty bite, tempered with the warm humour of its inhabitants at sunny gables in long evenings of nordic sunshine, where greed is merely thrift in wise disguise and generosity lurks in sly smiles, where folk are anxious to please and their lust for living is as strong as their roots in the soil. My ain folk after all, though I have dramatised their lives for a wider audience.

Here we decided to have tea in the car, and as I couldn't find a layby I backed into a field gate and broke the exhaust pipe, much to my annoyance, and I will have to see about getting it repaired. All the same it was a wonderful outing in the country of our courting days, Jane and I, in the land of Aikey Brae and Gavin Greig, for back in 1933 we were fee'ed and worked together on the farm of Newton of Kinmundy, THE DOOKIT FAIRM of my stories, where we fell in love and married when we left in December 1934. Today we scarched in the woods for Kinmundy House but couldn't find it. Perhaps it has been demolished to save taxes. But what with the beauty of the autumn woods and the sanctity of the churches we visited it was well worth a broken silencer at the end of the day, for it could have been much worse on these busy roads. When Jane and I were courting there was little else on the roads but bicycles and horse carts, and an occasional bus; but now danger lurks at every corner and cross-roads and we never thought to see such drastic changes in our lifetime. Indeed we never thought the world would change, but would remain always as it was then, if we thought about it at all. But it has changed and I suppose we should be thankful we are still alive together to see it.

December 5th, Thursday

Our thirty-fourth wedding anniversary and the first we have spent in the house without the children; the first time we have been without at least one of them since the first year of our marriage. So now Jane and I are back where we started, childless in a silent home, except that we are much better acquainted with each other than we were on that long distant

December day thirty-four years ago, when we set up house together in the midst of our youth, in the cottar house at Newseat of Peterhead, where Eric our oldest son was born fifteen months later, on the third of March, 1936, on the farm belonging to the late Mr. Robert Davidson, uncle of my present employer, Mr. Norman Davidson, at Aikenshill of Foveran.

It was a hard life for Jane and I in those days, as indeed it was for most working people, but even in our poverty and drudgery we had our moments of bliss which would be hard to recapture without the aid and incentive of youth. In our later years we can look back on those early days of our marriage with a wonder that we survived its harsher eventualities, and now we lock the door at night on our three sons, trusting they have something less to endure of adversity than we ourselves encountered.

December 25th, Wednesday

The things people send me at Christmas time! Would you believe it? Actually, because of our travels, or rather, as a direct result of them, I have in my possession, at this moment, one of the visitors' books from the atomic power station at Dounreay, in Caithness, sent to me for examination by Mr. Willie Sinclair of Bonar Bridge, one-time guide at the establishment and now employed by the Tourist Board, and whom I met while on holiday in Sutherlandshire, see entry for August 1st. Some of the remarks jotted down by visitors are quite amusing and I have copied out some of the briefest—

17.5.62. "All this—and a Viking poet to show you round". Dr. D. G. Gordon, Coldwells, Inverurie. (At one time our family physician.)

9.6.62. "I hope I'm not around when the Haggis goes up!" W.S.L.G.

9.6.62. "A most clear, concise explanation, given as 'the man in the street' can appreciate and understand it. A guide I would certainly like to spend more time with. He is proud of his country and heritage". Eric Robinson (The Eric Robinson?)

11.7.62. "Delighted to find I'm almost non-radioactive!" Burnibank, Hamilton.

12.7.62. "I shall never think of Dounreay without seeing our kilted guide with the charming manner". Melene Duncan, Sinclairtown Schoolhouse, Kirkcaldy.

22.7.62. "Ban the Bomb!" J.R.T.

8.8.62. "Just what I wanted to know!" Guy Burgess (Who spied for Russia).

8.8.62. "I hope it's all worth the expense" Aberdonian.

27.8.62. "If only I'd known!" Adolph Hitler.

7.6.63. "I wonder if the mist helps to keep the reactor cool headed?" (unsigned).

3.7.63. "Oh what a beautiful kilt!" G.J.C.

9.7.63. "Keep checking the valves". Pessimist!

20.7.63. "It'll never replace steam!" James Watt.

30.7.63. "Does the plutonium lose its flavour on the bed-post overnight?" J.W.

30.7.63. "I've a reactor at home but I call it wife". Doug.

31.7.63. "Can you make lighter fuel here?" Anon.

31.7.63. "The price of electricity still goes up".

31.8.63. "What is a fast reactor?" (Curious).

4.9.63. "Progress! May God grant that we think clearly and act wisely". R. Dodd.

25.6.64. "Ah now 'tis a pity about the mermaids". J. Bain.

24.7.64. "Since having helped to build this station it's fine to see the fruits of your labour actually in operation". J. McGibbon.

28.7.64. "Judge not this place by outward show. The feather floats but the pearl lies low". H. McCallum, Accrington, Lancs.

21.8.64. "Wonderful exhibition. The lilt in your voice is music itself". Angus and Mary Goodall, Newburgh, Fife.

25.8.64. "Bloody fine, especially the hot-water pipes". (A half-drowned camper).

24.6.65. "The little thing called man is gradually mastering the giants that have lived in the earth since it began". E. Blackhurst, London.

26.8.65. "Something out of Doctor Who?"

10.9.65. "They're a Weird Mob". A visiting Australian.

23.5.66. ". . . wish the giants and the mermaids were still here though!" Thank you Mister Guide. G. Richmond.

2.8.66. "This Atom Station rears its head, It's radiation belt expands, About this monster cased in lead, Acclaimed throughout the land . . ." J.N.P.

December 26th, Thursday

Letter to Mr. Wm. Sinclair of "Blandfield", Bonar Bridge, Sutherland.

Dear Mr. Sinclair,

Thank you for a most delightful letter, written with feeling and understanding, wisdom and the wealth of years, and all your enclosures, which I have enjoyed immensely. I have read your letter twice and found new joy in the second perusal. Indeed you are one of my best correspondents, and on the day I got yours I had another from a Swedish schoolmaster, written within a few miles of the Arctic Circle, and which I am enclosing, as a sort of experiment, to see what you think of my correspondents, of whom I have several.

Did you really have the Beatles at Dounreay? And is it the real Eric Robinson, the musical director who signs himself on June 9th, 1962? May 9th '62 marks the visit of our old local doctor (now retired and living near Inverurie) Dr. D. G. Gordon—a most refined and enlightened personage who used to take an avid interest in my literary endeavours. Of course I can understand that some of the signatures are fictitious, and that the appropriateness of others have been used with remarkable wit in taking full advantage of coincidence—"It'll never replace steam", for instance, by James Watt is a stunning gem, but I just can't believe that you had a visit from Adolph Hitler, in whatever disguise. But if the Beatles and the Luvers are genuine it would "sell" an article to the Press. "The Beatles at Dounreay", "Is Hitler Still Around?" or something of the sort, and of course I would have to mention Willie Sinclair as my confidante, and no doubt there are a great many readers who would remember you. Obviously you were highly respected in this vocation and I can imagine that you deserved each and every commendation, and that you were a natural choice for the part. I can also believe that you enjoyed your work, and that you are also devoted to the "Centre" at Bonar Bridge, and I can scarcely imagine you in any other role. With the appeal of youth and the wisdom of years you have developed your gift to the point of genuis, and for a man who has done so much for his country I think you deserve it. But why abandon the kilt? One can see that it is noticed with interest and would undoubtedly prove an asset to the Tourist Board.

I find great delight in recording the things in life that have given me greatest pleasure (which should make my diaries good reading) but I have also noted the sad things of which all life is a part. My diaries are voluminous and in quantity would compare favourably with those of Pepys or Evelyn, or even Boswell, but whether posterity will judge likewise about the quality of my endeavours is a matter of conjecture.

Nothing could give me more pleasure than letting you read some of my work, but in the meantime my papers are hardly in a state for presentation. But I shall shortly send you my book of quotations, choice gems of journalism which I have copied out for amusement, not really academic, but chosen for a certain poetical quality which I perceive in most forms of literature.

Writing of this area brings me to the mention of place names, which seems to be one of your interests, a very amusing and interesting hobby, though I only glance at it in passing.

As for Aikenshill: I don't know who the Aiken was but I feel that he goes well back into history. He may have been a sort of Thane or clan chief in control of the rising ground which the farm now occupies, an area of some 400 acres arable. The farm buildings are sited on the summit of the hill, which appears to have been a fort, probably about the time that your ancestors were occupying the Brochs. Some years ago, while excavating a silage pit, we came across an old ditch or earthworks skirting the brae, and I am told that the hill was mined for copper in the 13th century. It was blasted with dynamite for stone clearance about 16 years ago but nothing was discovered to strengthen this theory.

Like yourself I am rather selective in my T.V. programmes but we must respect the pleasure of others who seem to enjoy it, or whose minds may not have developed on the same lines as our own, the benefit of which is understood by each individual only, according to his or her experience, and which, under discussion, only leads to argument. I have several other hobbies, such as listening to popular light music and Country and Western songs on gramophone records, and the taping of my favourites on the recorder. I am also an ardent cinema-goer and vitally interested in dramatic art and criticism—though not in the local concert parties in the village halls. I have kept scrapbooks since 1945 and the house is stored with a vast resource of knowledge collected over the years.

My interest in politics was stronger in my youth than it is now and my favourite politician used to be the late A. Duff-Cooper, because he had in him the spirit of the poet, a spirit which was stifled when his father looked up the salary of the current poet-laureate—so it was straightway into politics for young Duff-Cooper. He relates his experience quite delightfully in OLD MEN FORGET, which for me was a literary treat.

But to change the subject—what with the new pulp mill at Fort William,* the proposed smelter at Invergordon, and the flourishing holiday and winter sports centre at Aviemore—what with all these amenities up north you shouldn't have much to complain about, and you've still got a railway to Wick and Thurso, Glasgow to Fort William and Mallaig, Dingwall to Kyle of Lochalsh, Inverness to Aberdeen and Perth—while we have scarcely a siding left in Buchan, and they've even closed the Royal Deeside line to Ballater. I don't know that the S.N.P. is all that good, unless they could retrieve the whisky duty, a subject which is always discreetly avoided in their arguments, but the augmentation of which alone might enable us to stabilise a Scottish currency. Indeed I have been informed that the present cash value in bonded whisky is greater than the gold bullion in the Bank of England. On the other hand a belligerent England may charge us more for household coal and deny us a market for our beef and cereals. But I suppose we could retaliate by denying them the benefit of Dounreay and the great water-power projects when these are switched to feed the English grid system. One has to think carefully about these things before putting down a cross for the S.N.P., and I'm still the canny Scot, not the rash Jacobite. Come to that I think our countrymen were fools to waste their nationhood on the extravagant Stuarts. Indeed I feel that with a few exceptions the Stuart Royalty were a bunch of pompous

* Even while I was typing the above sentence the major oil companies were test-drilling in the North Sea, though I never imagined their speculation would materialise with such repercussion in the Scottish Highlands.

wastrels and that any romance surrounding them was written with the blood of our over loyal forebears. Being a Highlander yourself I believe you will want to murder me for this, but if I am any judge of character at short acquaintance I believe you are a man of integrity and honour and would yourself have been reluctant, and would have considered your circumstances deeply before you threw your life away for the Jacobites (unless you are an adherent) or had been the serf of some cocksure laird or feudal chief and had to fecht for Charlie by compulsion, against your better judgement. But of course in all this I am being wise after the event—225 years after—all the same I'd still be wary of joining the S.N.P. so late in history—when all else is commercial amalgamation and small nations are becoming a danger to the peace of the world, a world gradually becoming too precarious for parochial strife, where even the mention of nationalism becomes a breeding ground for anarchy and terrorism.

The best description of northern Scotland I have ever read is in a book called IN SCOTLAND AGAIN, by H. V. Morton, in the middle pages, and somewhere else he tells us that America's Wild West was fully discovered before the Scottish Highlands were even explored, and that before the '45 rebellion Lowlanders went north at the peril of their lives, and usually under the greatest compulsion or expediency, and usually made their wills before setting out. It was not until Dr. Johnson's TOUR OF THE HEBRIDES, and after Boswell's publication of that itinerary that ordinary people began to enjoy the Highlands of Scotland, and of course the coming of the railways made that pleasure available for most people.

I have before me an old coaching guide for 1827 which informs me that Bonar Bridge (I mean the actual bridge) was built by the heritors of Sutherland at the expense of £13,791 Sterling; that it consists of three arches, the centre one of iron, 150 feet, the two others of stone, each 110 feet, and that traffic over the bridge brought great improvement to your area, especially from the south, and that "excellent farms are now seen, where, a few years ago, only wretched crofts and black huts were visible". I also have a copy of BLACK's GUIDE TO SCOTLAND for 1880, with a railway itinerary and a whole chapter devoted to Sutherland and one for Caithness. By the way did you know that Caithness got its name from the Keith's, the Earl Marischals of Scotland, who originally came from Germany? Exiled from the continent they settled on the east coast of Scotland under the name of Katti, thus: Katti— Kath—Kathness—Caithness—Keth—Keith. The Keiths were staunch Jacobites and after the '15 rebellion were disinherited for joining with the Earl of Mar. Ironically they fled to Prussia, from whence they came, and the last Earl Marischal died in the armed services of Frederick the Great. But no doubt the Kaths left some good fighting men in the Highlands of Scotland; the "women from Hell", as the Germans themselves called them after a bayonet charge in the trenches by the kilted Scots during the First World War.

etc., etc.,

Sincerely,
D. Toulmin.

1969

Granny died today in Foresterhill Hospital, Aberdeen, aged 78 years past August 5th last year, surviving my father by twenty years less 18 days. None of us saw her die. She died amongst strangers and yet I was relieved that I wasn't present. I never wanted to see my poor old mother die and I was granted that wish. Sister Cook of Ward One broke it to me gently over the 'phone at the farm. I had just come from the muddy fields with my tractor and a load of turnips, when I was told to go to the 'phone in the farmhouse. I rang Sister Cook and waited . . . oh so long it seemed, maybe three minutes—what were they going to tell me? That mother was worse? That I must come at once before the end? And then . . . "We don't like having to break the news to relatives in this manner. I am very sorry . . . very sorry indeed Mr. Reid, but I have to inform you that your mother passed on just after lunch, when she had eaten quite heartily: rather sudden; we didn't expect it just yet, but she was scarcely aware of it; there was no struggle, she didn't suffer, I can assure you of that. We were going to send for you today anyhow; just to tell you how ill your mother really was, but we didn't have time, even we were surprised at the end—it was so very sudden." So now it was over. Granny was dead at last. How long I have dreaded this day and now it was here. How often have I waved Goodbye and wondered if it would be the last time I would see her alive. But till now there has always been another time. Last night was our last meeting with her but I didn't believe it: The doctor had said she would last another two or three weeks and this was only a few days . . .

I got the death certificate from the general office at the hospital: "Cardiac Congestion, caused by recurrent Chronic Bronchitis". The doctor, John Gaddie, was sympathetic and tried to explain the cause of Granny's death; of how the lungs were damaged and were not oxygenising the blood, which laboured the heart and starved the brain, causing Granny to haver a lot of nonsense in her conscious moments, some of it (he said) characteristic of her Scottish parentage and environment, and not without its humour in the Doric, even on her death bed.

My sister had broken her ankle on the ice a few days previously. She was on crutches and wanted to take our mother's body back to Stonehaven. It would cost us £20 more and I said I couldn't afford it. I wanted to leave her body in the rest rooms at the Undertaker's place in the city. What did it matter now? But Flora offered to pay the £20 because she said mother's neighbours would want to see her corpse. So we compromised with £10 each and mother's body would go back to Stonehaven.

Later in the evening I contacted the gravedigger at Old Deer, which was no easy matter, because I had forgotten his name, and couldn't get his number in the telephone directory, so we had to go to the police at Lodge Walk. They said it was not their affair, and that we should have contacted the County Police at Bucksburn, but they helped us just the same—as if it mattered where we went. Opening of the grave would cost us £18, mother not being a ratepayer in the Old Deer parish. Twenty years ago I buried my father for 30/- and £3 for the burial ground, which we wouldn't have to buy this time as mother would go in the same grave.

Next day, Thursday, we called at the bank in Aberdeen and took out all of Granny's savings for nearly twenty years, having been in my name for three years as a trustee against this time of her death. In my earlier diaries (November 11th, 1950) you can read where my mother sent me a cheque for £50, which was later increased to £76 . . . "to put me away", as she said in a letter, "and the sooner it's on your hands the better as we never know what might happen to me as I am getting old and not very strong at times". Thus she had entrusted to me her funeral expenses nearly twenty years before her death, which will enable us to meet all our commitments. At any rate she made sure she would not die in debt. An oak coffin will cost us £39. I would have settled for pine at £29, and the undertaker agreed that it was sufficient, but my sister insisted on having the best for our mother, and of course I agreed accordingly.

Burns' Birthday, January 25th was Granny's funeral day. The Rev. Robert Richmond of Stonehaven was blind, having lost his sight during the war in Malaya—and my sister Flora was on crutches with her broken ankle, while the undertaker, Mr. "Jock" Sheppard was like a character out of a Dickens' novel (Mr. Micawber if you like, or even Mr. Pickwick) and you never did see such a splendid funeral. I led the Rev. Richmond to the graveside to give the service, making sure he didn't go too near the edge of the hole (for obvious reasons) and then took his arm gently back to our car again.

Granny's four stalwart grandsons carried her coffin shoulder high into Old Deer cemetery, young Kenneth and Edward Coutts on my sister's side and our Jack and Graham for us, the knowledge of which would have made her feel very proud indeed, and I am sure it impressed our relatives, who may not have realised that Granny had nurtured such grandsons, not including our Eric, away in far Malaysia. I was much honoured by the presence of her youngest and only surviving brother at the graveside, my uncle and senior by three years, and I made sure he got a cord with the others to lower his oldest sister into her last dark residence. There was water in the grave and we had to wait at the gate until the sexton ladled it out with a pan before we could approach with the corpse. I looked into the earthen hole and saw the lid of my father's coffin, slightly bent in the middle, where it had lain there these twenty years, in this damp hole. Over the years I have brought mother here to kneel and pray for my father, and to shed a quite tear on the flowers she had brought him, and often as I stood aside I have wondered when her turn would come to be laid at rest with him. Twenty years are a long time in passing but it is here at last.

Everyone was impressed with the Rev. Richmond. His words at the house in Barclay Street (my sister's residence) were comforting and full of feeling and touched the mourners deeply, even to the mentioning of the little child soon to be born to my sister's daughter, Frances Cheyne, the young life that Granny would never see, much as she was looking forward to it. On the evening that Jock Sheppard brought the corpse he told us some of the most weird and amusing stories of his career as an undertaker that I have ever heard, and all the time banging the table in the kitchen with his huge fist and prodding my sister with his hard, vicious fingertips, until he nearly had

118

her off her chair, what with her broken ankle and unsure of her balance, and all the time his eyes popping and his laugh exploding until he had us all out of our grief and almost oblivious of mother's stiffened body stretched out in the other room. He was the classic tragi-comedian who made bereavement seem like a period of unreality, while the Rev. Richmond sat on another chair, smiling benignly, until someone called at the door to take him home.

I was really delighted to meet this worthy pair, the Rev. Richmond and Jock Sheppard the undertaker, two of the most unlikely individuals for their respective tasks and yet the most efficient when the time came for them to act, which they did professionally. I took one for a visiting farmer, the Rev. Richmond I recall, and Jock Sheppard for an auctioneer, and wondering what the devil the two of them could have to do with our mother's funeral, until my sister introduced us. I thought perhaps they were two acquaintances paying their last respects, which shows how little I knew of my mother's affairs, though I have since recalled that she used to mention the joiner who mended her windows and sink board, an humorous local character I would have considered long gone from the community, a survivor from a more colourful past, invested with all the Victorian splendour, solemnity, dignity and decorum which made Granny's funeral one of distinction in the Mearns capital. I had been proved wrong in my sister's choice of these gentlemen to officiate at our mother's interment and later glad that I yielded to hcr arrangements.

Before Granny could be shown to the neighbours her corpse had to be brought back to normal temperature and all her blood drained off, replacing it with a red dye which brought back the roses of youth to her cheeks and a natural smoothness to her skin, like a waxen effigy out of Madame Tussaud's, warm with the colours of the flowers around her that the neighbours had brought. This reincarnation cost us a further £5 and made mother seem like a bride out of Frankenstein's laboratory, but of course it was performed on a hospital slab, and had to be decided upon by my sister at short notice, and on her own initiative, because I couldn't be contacted—but the pathologists warned her that unless she agreed to it mother would be discoloured in her coffin.

Most people would naturally object to this procedure and would prefer not to exhibit the corpse rather than agree to it. But we were afraid that Granny's sisters (our aunts) would take offence unless we made her presentable—although we needn't have bothered, because only two out of five turned up for the funeral, the others proffering illness or distance as a reason for their absence. Yet I was surprised to see so many people call at the house, 81 Barclay Street, and even moreso at the graveyard, where a lot of people were waiting, fortunately in the sunshine, mostly my wife's people, and old man Willox and old man Coutts, 80 and 82 years old respectively, both smoking their pipes and looking most sympathetic after the interment. I was sorry that for lack of time I couldn't bring these two veterans, these two heads of family to a handshake, though I greeted both individually, one on each side of the gate, like clan chiefs surrounded by their families. My sister by the way is married into the Coutts family, and Mr. Willox is my wife's father.

I had driven from Stonehaven to Old Deer in front of the hearse because the driver didn't know the way, and he told me not to go beyond thirty miles an hour. My uncle sat beside me while Jane was in the back seat between the Rev. Richmond and top-hatted Mr. Sheppard. On the return journey I discovered that our blind minister was a chain smoker and fairly liberal with his hand out of cigarettes, so much so that on several occasions I politely refused his offer, especially so when I was at the driving wheel with all their lives in my hands. Jock Sheppard didn't smoke, still living in an era before cigarettes were invented, or at least before they became popular or fashionable, but he listened intently while I talked over my shoulder to the minister in the back seat, rather mystified I think at the talk of mythology and legend that went on between myself and the clergyman. Being a stranger locally, the Rev. Richmond had no knowledge whatsoever of Old Deer and its religious associations: from Pagan orgies to Christian conversion by Saint Drostan; the Book of Deir or its famous abbey, or indeed that the district of Deer had been the cradle of Christianity in the land of Brude and the pictish tribes who had danced round the Druids' stone circle on the summit of Aikey Brae. My companion in theology knew nothing of these things, but in his world of darkness I tried meekly to shed as much light as I could on their origins and influences in our part of the country.

On arrival back at Stonehaven I left Jane and Jock Sheppard at my sister's place and drove round to the manse in Cameron Street with the Rev. Richmond, passing his church on the way where my late mother attended. I wanted to tell him of all the beautiful things I had read in the wayside pulpits; of how the very heart of me took flight on the wings of Hebrew poetry— of how I sneaked into empty churches on Sunday afternoons to see from where the minister had taken his text, and how often it had seemed to me that the Bible had been left open for me at the very chapter and verse from which I should read, it was so appropriate to my mood and circumstances of the moment—and how I liked to read alone in God's empty house, in the stillness and silence of eternity, where the sacred scripture elevated my thoughts in joyful veneration. I did so like the Rev. Richmond (whatever he thought of my conceit for myself—which was purely unintentional) but there was no time to open my mind further to him in the circumstances. So I got my blind friend out of the car and led him by the arm to the manse door, where he said he would manage, though his wife was out shopping he told me, and when we parted I left with his blessing.

The last hour I spent with my mother alone was in Barclay Street (my sister's place) Stonehaven, before she was removed to hospital for the last time. I think she knew it was her death bed and she said she would rather like to be away from it all, though she said it cheerfully, with no sign of remorse or tears. She was being very brave I thought, while she spread her knitting on the bed quilt, showing me what had to be done to the garment, a cardigan I believe it was, the colour of the buttons she had chosen for it and for whom it was intended. She was not supposed to be smoking but she took a packet of hidden cigarettes from under her pillow and asked me for a light. I struck a match for her but she could only take a few drags before the coughing started and she had to put out the fag, saving it she said for her last moments, as if it would give her courage to die with a fag in her lips, a solace which would certainly be denied her in hospital, and more likely to be replaced with an oxygen mask. I had to take her up to the chamber pot, where she stood in a tremble, and would have fallen from weakness but for my support, and I got her back to bed again, breathless but smiling in her usually tolerant battle with life—and this time with death itself. When eventually told of her death I wept in my wife's arms with the shamelessness of an overgrown schoolboy.

February 7th, Friday

A fearful snowstorm and the main road like a standing goods train of stranded vehicles. We buried grandma just in time, on a day of brilliant sunshine. A week later we were engulfed in blinding snow blizzards and all the roads blocked, so that we wouldn't have got near the cemetery, nearly fifty miles distant from Stonehaven.

Tonight we gave shelter to an old but gentlemanly farmer, Mr. William Barclay of Mains of Crichie, Stuartfield, but now living in retirement with his wife at the Terrace, Longside, while his farm is managed by his married and only son, Bill Barclay jnr. When he reached our door (as Jane tells me, because I was in the byre at the time) Mr. Barclay, who is 74, assisted by a stranded lorry driver, was in a state of collapse, suffering as he does from chronic bronchitis, and being without a necessary reserve of the tablets prescribed to relieve his respiratory congestion. He had merely gone to the marts in the city for the day and had no thought or premonition of being stormbound. As he sat gasping on a chair Jane was afraid that he would die on her hands, but after a cup of strong warm tea he revived and said he would be all right after a rest from the blizzard.

During the evening, while the snow battered the windows and the wind moaned in the chimney, I talked with Mr. Barclay on the methods and economics of agriculture, besides touching on world topics in general. A veteran of the first World War, when he endured a whiff of poison gas, from which he still suffers, Mr. Barclay has a pleasing kenspeckle personality and he proved quite easy to talk to. But his sole interest is farming and I found it difficult to interest him in any other subject under the sun.

He slept overnight in our bedroom with the electric blanket while Jane and I bedded down on the settee in front of the fire in our small living room-cum-kitchen. Next day, because of his bronchial condition, we were greatly relieved at noon when Mr. Barclay's son appeared with a Land-rover to take his father home. We had phoned from the farm to inform his family where the old man was, knowing they would be anxious for his safety overnight; a night that will be remembered by a great many stranded farmers and business men who slept in cottar houses by the roadside. Before leaving us the old man expressed his appreciation for our hospitality and pressed two £1 notes into Jane's hand, at the same time patting her on the shoulder, as if she were his own daughter—"for being so good to me, lass", he said.

Even though it was Saturday I was working all day, first outside and then in the byre, because of the storm and scarcity of hands. After supper we dragged Mr. Barclay's car, a Singer Gazelle, out of the snow-drift and into one of our fields to let the snowploughs get through. It was a heavy job and we had to use two tractors to move the car on the hard packed ice, using headlights in the pitch dark. We also had to drag the milk tanker to the top of the farm brae, because he got stuck in the snow, which turned to ice under his spinning rear wheels. But we were glad to see him because the bulk tank at the farm was lipping full with 625 gallons of perishable milk, and some of it had been poured into emergency plastic containers, which had to be split open to let the tanker pipe suck it out. When the tanker had gone a lorry load of draff came slithering up the farm road in the dark, without our assistance, in a howling, whirling snow blizzard; but we merely showed the driver where to topple it in the draff-shed and went home, for by now we were weary and fagged out in the struggle.

Sad to say, within the year, or rather, before the year was out, we heard that poor Mr. Barclay's wife and brother had been killed near their home in a car crash, while his son and daughter-in-law were injured, the woman severely, so much so that the young couple had to give up the farm completely. Perhaps Mr. Barclay was spared the full severity of the blow, for a recent stroke had rendered him incapable of grasping the knowledge of the tragedy, or being aware of the funerals.

Little did we think that stormy night when he sat in our humble little cottage that this old man was on the threshold of such a fate. And he had just been telling us how much he depended on his devoted wife. He himself died some few months after the tragedy.

February 9th, Sunday

The snowstorm continues, but now with a break between the blizzards. Aikenshill is a farm of bleak exposure, completely devoid of shelter for man or beast, a cruel but healthy residence, where the north wind on the farm brae cuts your breath, numbs your cheeks and chills your extremities, so that sometimes I can scarcely face it, but have to turn my back to the blast and walk backwards, or sling a jacket over my head, holding it tight around my neck to shield my cheek bones from the stinging hail showers.

I have been so much on edge lately that I couldn't get started to anything seriously. My typewriter lies idle in a corner while I walk the floor, glad to be out of the blizzards whistling at the windows. But at any hour (even on Sunday) I may be called upon with my Dexta tractor to help pull a beleaguered milk tanker or a lorry or even a car up the steep brae to the farm, so that I cannot settle my mind to routine thinking.

Thank heaven for television, for in the evening we watched Gary Cooper in an old Western called THE HANGING TREE, something I couldn't have done on the snowbound farms of yesteryear, when I had to cycle nearly ten miles both ways for such a treat.

February 10th, Monday

We have been all day with shovels and tractor snowplough on the farm brae and also digging out silage for cow feed, now under a foot of snow. The snow had stopped blowing but a keen frost gave it a crisp edge, so that it wouldn't leave our shovels. After a tiring day, with my back muscles aching, and just after tea, we had to start up our tractors again in the dark and drag another tanker up from the main road, where he got stuck in a wheel spin on the hard packed snow. He syphoned out another 583 gallons of milk from our bulk tank, some of it in cans, which were tipped in during the process. The present daily yield is around 470 gallons.

The next day I grubbed the snow on the farm road with spring-toothed harrows, smashing it up for the foreman to sweep it aside with the snow plough. The traffic is moving again but huge banks of snow are piled up on both sides of the main road, though sunshine and a freshening wind are helping things considerably.

It was a lengthy snowstorm however, for nearly three weeks later, on the 1st of March I was writing thus to Mr. Willie Sinclair of Bonar Bridge: "I am typing this by the fireside on a Sunday afternoon of howling wind and driving sleet, and such a comfort it is to view it from the window rather than endure its bite from a tractor cab. In these last weeks I have been numbed with cold, scarcely able to command my feet on the control pedals, and whatever they teach in the agricultural colleges it will never improve this aspect of farming. It is an environment which has to be endured rather than learned, and time or practice makes no improvement on one's ability to cope with it, rather the opposite as the heat of one's body grows less with advancing years.

"I look out upon frozen fields that fringe upon the sand dunes and surging sea, awash with white as it churns the shore; and overhead a sky of hammered lead, which looks as if it could never again be burnished by a summer sun. But at least I am better off than the early lambs that cower for shelter under their mother's bellies, where the wool is a tangle of matted ice and the teats are raw with cold."

Alas we had to wait another three months for a blink of summer, the first hint we had of taking the road again, Jane and I, with most of the spring work behind us and some prospect of a holiday. Our first venture of the year was a run to Dunnottar Castle, sea-girt fortress on its green knoll of red sandstone rock just south of Stonehaven, stronghold of the Keiths for so many years and finally destroyed by Cromwell in his efforts to subdue Scotland. Some of the Scottish Covenanters were imprisoned here in 1685, when 122 men and 45 women were confined to the Whigs' Vault, where they endured three months of privation and hunger in the most obscene circumstances of filth and torture, a martyrdom commemorated by a list of their names in Dunnottar churchyard. The present war memorial is situated on a plateau overlooking the rock, where Cromwell sited his cannon to bombard the castle during the siege of 1651.

Jane gathered some wild primroses on the green slopes of the castle rock and we uprooted a few to try them in the garden. Today the sea was green and calm but the resident keeper said it had been a winter of terrible storms that shook the mighty rock on which the castle stands. When we had examined the ruins we walked hand in hand back up the steep path to the keeper's lodge on the main road, where we had tea in the car, and then off to the old parish church at Kinneff, white and beautiful in a green hollow by the sea, quiet among its old leaning gravestones, lichened with age and the names of their inhabitants washed away by the rains of many long forgotten winters.

We walked quietly among the dead on the carpet of grass, while the white gulls came sailing over the tree-tops, carried by the wind on outstretched wings, mewing their surprise at the sight of us. Inside the old church was as quiet as a mouse scratch and the plaster peeling from the walls. Here the Rev. Granger and his wife hid the Scottish Regalia which she had smuggled out of Dunnottar Castle in a clothes basket under the noses of Cromwell's helmeted guards. A fine moulding of the Scottish crown, sword and sceptre projects from the wall, marking the spot where they were concealed for eight years under the floor boards, until the restoration of Charles II. I feel that a visit to Dunnottar Castle is incomplete unless one sees the lonely old kirk at Kinneff by the seashore, where you can stand before the pulpit over the spot where the jewelled crown was deposited. This is not the original building, but unless something is done soon to preserve the present church this historic site will soon fall to pieces.

June 1st, Sunday

We motored to Deeside, where there was yet snow on the mountains though there were green leaves on the trees, and the lovely geans white with blossom. We looked in by at Braemar Castle, impressive from without but less interesting inside than I had expected, and certainly not worth the three shillings we were each charged for admission. The castle is a pill-box, turreted structure of baronial style with star-shaped curtain walls pierced with gun-loops, obviously for the use of cross-fire under attack or siege, and the building in excellent condition. The castle is still occupied by the Farquharson family and closely associated with the raising of the Stuart Standard on "the Braes o' Mar", on behalf of the Old Pretender in 1715, by the Earl of Mar. It was reconstructed as a fort by the English Government in 1747 and garrisoned by Redcoats like Corgarff for 50 years to prevent further uprising among Jacobite sympathisers. Around 1831 the Farquharsons reclaimed their old mansion as a residence and still occupy the upper storeys of the castle.

June 29th, Sunday

We motored to Druminnor Castle, near Rhynie village and the hill named Tap o' Noth, home of the late Lady Margaret Forbes-Sempill, who was lately killed in a road accident, after she had spent many years of labour, personally restoring the castle of her ancestors. She had just completed the renovation work when the fatality occurred, and the castle is now a lovely shade of rain-washed pink, very light pastel, like the colour of a fading rose petal, which is very beautiful in the spring in a setting of budding trees.

There is much to interest one here in the cellars, where material for an agricultural museum has been assembled, from early cooking utensils and domestic appliances to primitive farming hand-tools, some of them still in use when I started work on the land. Most striking of these was a flail-thresher, used by hand; a fiddle-sower and a "Bobbin' John", a hand instrument for sowing turnip, kale or vegetable seeds. But I was more interested in the general, or shall we say more sophisti-cated furnishings in the great hall of the castle, particularly a French painting of a ruined palace on a rock, perhaps near Rouen, reputed to be the birthplace of William the Conqueror in 1027, whom I have since learned was so obese from long debauchery that his bloated corpse disintegrated in sewage after death and could scarcely be contained in a coffin, an incidence which has almost destroyed my romantic vision of the conquering hero who changed the history and architecture of England; an ugly stain on the red flag of old Normandy, emblazoned with golden leopards when it flaunted the breeze on Jumieges Abbey, consecrated when a triumphant William returned from England in the year after the conquest.

Another painting, that of the late Lady Forbes-Sempill at the age of nine was strikingly life-like and beautiful, soft as the fall of a flower petal, and in one of the bedrooms a portrait of her mother as a young woman, delicate and colourful as the wings of a butterfly. But my greatest fascination was a set of opera glasses presented to one of the family by Napoleon III. Here was optical science in the theatre, the first "close-up" of a performing artist on the stage, though mostly used I suppose for scanning the galleries and spying on the private boxes rather than what they were intended for.

The glasses were small and dainty, obviously intended for female use, inlaid with highly coloured miniature figures in polished enamel finish, typical of the period of the brocaded sleeve in high society, the crinoline skirt, wasp-waist and bustle and the bee-hive hair-style, or whatever was fashionable at the time.

Miss Joan Wright, custodian of the castle, observing my interest in the glasses, took them from the glass cabinet and allowed me to have a peep through them, whereupon I directed my gaze upon a crinolined lady in a corner of the museum, which took me back a hundred years or so. Here in the great hall there is an entrancing display of period costumes and ladies' fashions of a former century, purporting that a strict diet was even more important in those days than it is now, for how other could they get inside those incredible corsets unless they hungered themselves considerably. Thus hampered and tight-laced the society ladies of the eighteenth and nineteenth centuries were less prudent in matters of personal hygiene, however sedate and well-mannered, so they walked upon the "scented lawns" of the wealthy landowners, where a type of grass was sown which exuded a pleasant fragrance when crushed by the foot, like a certain genus of plants when squeezed in the finger-tips, and thus reducing the risk of "B.O.". And of course we must consider the inadequate plumbing of those days and the inconvenience of frequent bathing. "Ring of Confidence" my foot! All a lot of mouthwash!

Druminnor is an old stronghold of the Clan Forbes, where they feuded for generations with the Gordons, their strongest rivals in this area of Aberdeenshire, and the story is told of how they tried to settle their differences by peaceful means, something on the lines of the modern idiom that "if you can't beat 'em, join 'em", but in this case with rather distressing results for both parties. Forbes it appears invited the clan chief of the Gordons, and a number of his supporters, to come unarmed to Druminnor, to a feast at the banqueting table, where they could arrange a truce, Forbes assuring the Gordons that no harm would come to them under his roof. The Gordon chief, though somewhat suspicious, but anxious for peace, accepted the arrangement, and Forbes cautioned his own men to abide by their honour, that not a Gordon was to be harmed, but that they might keep their small weapons under cover in case of treachery. He would watch for this himself he said, and at the first sign of it he would stroke his beard, and his men could be on their guard.

So the lion sat down with the bear so to speak, and shared their prey, which was the venison and wine of the Druminnor estates, and the long feuding Forbes and Gordon clans were at last on speaking terms over the food-laden table in the great hall of the castle. When they had dined and wined to their satisfaction the hall was cleared for revelry, song music and dancing, and everybody was having a grand time, and the Gordon youths mixing with the damsels of the Forbes clan as if they had known each other all their lives.

Forbes took Gordon aside for a chat by the great marble fireplace, where the logs blazed away merrily and sent the little golden sparks sailing up the wide canopy which served as a mantelpiece. During their conversation Forbes became so engrossed with his late enemy's talk, of how he meant to improve his estates and so on, that he inadvertently, and quite unconsciously reverted to an old habit of his while amused or entertained—he stroked his beard, and lo, before he realised what was happening, his men had unsheathed their hidden dirks and fifteen of Gordon's unwary, surprised and quite defenceless Highlanders lay bleeding and dying on the floor.

So the Forbes and Gordon clans were back in square one, more bitter and revengeful than ever and the old feuding and fighting went on. The great hall where this accidental tragedy was enacted can still be seen in the castle of Druminnor, and the ghost of the Gordons still walks at night, appearing on the stroke of twelve, a long white figure stroking a flowing beard with a skeleton hand. Quite recently a local female journalist challenged the ghost of Druminnor, sleeping through the night in the dark room, and though she admitted it was a bit eerie, and that she heard some quite unusual sounds that startled her a little, the ghost never appeared.

On leaving Druminnor I went into three small churches, namely the diminutive ark-roofed Saint Mary's Episcopal Chapel at Rhynie, and the parish church of the same village. In Saint Drostane's church at Insch I was much taken with the multi-coloured window glazing and by a tapestry of the Last Supper on the wall, this last exhibit a masterpiece in detail, even to the beards of the disciples and the whites of the Master's eyes, and the loaves of bread upon the table, and the decor as lusciously coloured as new blown flowers. I read from the 39th Psalm, verses 4, 5 and 11: "Lord, make me to know mine end, and the measure of my days, what it is; that I may know how frail I am".

"Behold thou hast made my days as an handbreadth; and mine age is as nothing before thee: verily every man at his best state is altogether vanity. Selah."

"When thou with rebukes dost correct man for iniquity, thou makest his beauty to consume away like a moth: surely every man is vanity. Selah." And the poetry of the verses signified deeply in the empty church.

July 27th, Sunday

Today visited the excavation works on the pre-historic settlement of the Cullykhan peninsula, near Pennan, on the Moray Firth coast of Aberdeenshire. Earthworks and vitrified fortifications clearly visible where the turf has been removed, also pebbled floors and blackened hearth stones in the living quarters, where the flint-knappers squatted nearly three thousand years ago. Some interesting exhibits included a chisel of the bronze age, around 1000 B.C., fragments of pottery, stone tools, a jade bracelet, etc., and everything lucidly explained by the students of archaeology on the site. They have also exposed the foundations of a castle dating 1690, now clearly defined on the headland, and brickwork from Fort Fiddes, dating from the Jacobite disturbances, besides a cannon on the top of the cliff, probably aimed at the remnants of the Spanish Armada sailing round our northern coasts. There is even a gun-site here from World War II, proving the wisdom of using the headland as a defensive position from the days of the Viking invaders.

Down at the water's edge we scrambled through the Needle's Eye, a gigantic but narrow fissure in the cliff face directly below the ancient fortifications, penetrating the rock from a sort of side passage and emerging upon an enormous cavern facing the sea, obviously providing a terrific spectacle in a storm, when the giant waves come plunging into this awesome cavity, as far as the slit in the cliffs, or Needle's Eye, where we had entered from the beach. This phenomenal cave stands apart from the main cliff wall, not unlike the Fiddle-Bow rock at Portgordon, but larger by far and more terrifying in a boisterous sea. Jane and I skipped from rock to slippery rock while the tide was out, trying to reach the entrance and the open sea, but the water got deeper and the distance much further than we expected and we were forced to turn back. It is a place I should fear to be trapped in by a freak wave, but today the sea was hushed to a mere treble on the ebb tide, the foremost waves encircling the rocks in a gentle swell.

High above us the roof of the cavern was carved and grooved by the monstrous waves until it looked like the groined vaulting in some mighty cathedral of the Sea Gods, with here and there a mighty rock held in a crack like a pebble, but would crush you like a beetle if it fell. "Hell's Lum" was just beyond us on the cliff top at Troup Head, which is another spectacular phenomena in the area, but too far for us in the circumstances, so we gathered up some sea-shells on the strand before setting off in the car for the main road, along a narrow cart track which was now nearly bumper to bumper with the cars of curious sight-seers coming and going to the excavation works, with passing places rather far between.

August 14th, Thursday

We are on the second day of our holidays, Jane and I, and I am writing this in a layby on the road from Dunfermline to Crieff, somewhere between Rumbling Bridge and Gleneagles, close by the Devon River, where we slept a night in our old Austin A30 van some four years ago. Now of course we have our new Viva, but I can hear the murmur and music of the water through the open window of the car, just as we heard it that other night, and I have stopped for that precise purpose, to renew old experiences and past joys.

We are heading for Comrie, that sweet and gentle village nestling in the green velvet hills, where our camp is pitched at West Lodge caravan site, and we hope to remain there for the rest of the week. We came to Comrie by way of Perth and Crieff, resting in a layby directly opposite Ochtertyre House, that delightful residence of the Murray family, where I couldn't resist a photograph of such unobtainable beauty. That was yesterday, and in the evening we spent an absorbing hour at the arts and crafts exhibition in the old Parish Church at Comrie, which is now a centre for Youth Club activities. There was more than we could stomach in the short time available, especially in the older section of the display, which was more in the nature of a folk museum, and naturally devoted to the past life of the community, but also contained a varied assortment of old books, prints and pictures which I would have liked to study in much greater detail. But even in the new section I was much struck with some religious verses composed and set to music by a local girl (or woman) called Flora Cartwright, besides some floral work done in embroidery from the same hand, which is surely quite magnificent talent in one person. The verses of J. Henderson Macpherson, the local garage poet were also very much to my liking, typed sheets pinned to a board on the wall by his sister, because the bard himself was too shy to have them displayed or published.

Anyone familiar with Comrie will remember the old church as a white structure with a magnificent spire near the bridge on the river Earn, evidently popular with anglers, and a dream picture for the artist, as I could see from the exhibition, especially in winter, when the tree-clad slopes in the background are tinselled in snow.

Today we were conducted through Huntingtower Castle by a somewhat ebullient guide who was worth a shilling tip for the wealth of information he imparted to us, and to the two Australian girls who comprised our foursome on the castle roof and battlements. Apparently the castle was formerly known as Ruthven, but because of the treacherous record of its inheritors, and in particular concerning the implication of its owner in the Gowrie Conspiracy at Perth, he was disinherited and his estates confiscated by the crown and the castle sold under the name of Huntingtower. It stands just outside Perth on the road to Crieff and John Buchan borrowed merely the title for his novel HUNTINGTOWER and relates nothing of the castle's history. This I learned from our bombastic guide, who gave us such a dressing down on the family history, and on every moral and physical detail in its tradition, he certainly brought us into the picture of mediaeval life. He gave the key to one of the girls to open the main portal, referring to her as "Honey Bunch", while throughout the tour of the castle he addressed the other girl as "Tootie-Fruitie" or "Tweetie-Pie", which made them both smile generously without apparent embarrassment, and I'm sure they felt delightfully at home.

From here we motored to Loch Leven, near Kinross, where Mary Queen of Scots was imprisoned, but the water was too rough for a crossing to the castle, so we had to be content with looking at it from the old graveyard at the ferry, just as I remembered it from a photograph in my history book at school, but much nearer in focus than I saw it now.

We thoroughly enjoyed Dunfermline, especially the abbey, where we stood in reverence at the tomb of Robert the Bruce and spent half-an-hour on the marble statuary in this marvellous church. When we first opened the red padded door the beauty of the interior almost took our breath away: it was transporting; so elegant, so elevating in thought; this hymnary in stone, a hushed music in the presence of the Almighty, so that we crept along the aisles in subdued wonderment, humbled by the dedication of a faith in mankind for the glory of his creator.

133

Also interred here are Queen Margaret and Malcolm Canmore, Alexander I and his queen, David I and Malcolm IV. Outside we took some photos in the public gardens and pondered the ruins of the Royal Palace, near the abbey, the mediaeval capital of Scotland, where David II, James I and Charles I were born and where

"The King sits in Dunfermline toun
Drinking the Blude-red wine"

as the old ballad of Sir Patrick Spens tells us, before this unfortunate mariner set sail to fetch the Maid of Norway. Here also I marvelled at the splendour and decoration of the County Buildings and the wrought-iron fretwork gates at the entrance to Pittencrieff Glen—and everywhere the generous hand of Andrew Carnegie is in evidence, with £500,000 given to the town of his birth, and the result is money well spent. And of course I realise my own debt to Andrew Carnegie, for the public libraries he has made available for the poorer students of literature thirsting after knowledge.

While in Dunfermline I also met an old friend of my cinema going days whom I haven't seen for 25 years. He was Mr. George Gilchrist, now proprietor of the Kinema in Burntisland, but manager of the Regal cinema in Peterhead when I first met him in 1941. It was during the war; the black-out, the bombing and food rationing, when I got a free pass from Mr. Gilchrist every time I visited the cinema with a dozen eggs, which was about once a week; plus the price of my eggs at black market value, and up in his office he locked them in his safe like James Bond would stack hand grenades. Indeed I was almost back in the jam-jar era during the Hitler war, though the cinema was rocked occasionally by bomb blast. He also supplied me with the current cine literature—KINEMATOGRAPH WEEKLY and the DAILY FILM RENTER, my literary diet of those days, which eventually led me to Shakespeare and the English poets.

We were into our last moments in Dunfermline, on the point of returning to the Abbey car park, when I said to Jane I would ask at the nearest cinema if Mr. Gilchrist was still the manager there. So I turned about and was just approaching the Regal picture house when I met a gentleman I was sure I knew. He must have thought likewise, because he caught my enquiring glance and stopped, and I went back and asked if he was indeed Mr. Gilchrist? He said he was but that he almost failed to recognise me in passing, but when I gave my name we shook hands heartily and he expressed his pleasure in meeting me so unexpectedly. I thought that he had lost something of his old physique, which used to be that of an athlete, and indeed my friend had been a boxer before he entered the cinema world. The shoulders that used to bulge in a dress suit now sagged slightly in his mundane overalls, and his face had lost some of the gloss that used to shine over a bow-tie when he stood at the top of the carpeted stairs at the Regal cinema in Peterhead. Not that I usually take much notice of such things; but in my friend's case it showed that some of the glamour had rubbed off in the cinema business, and there was a hint of the mechanic in the slightly grained hands that were always so white and shiny under the lights on the auditorium roof. He seemed to read my thoughts, or perhaps he was conscious of my difficulty in recognising him after a quarter of a century, and he had aged just a little. Perhaps I wore a puzzled expression, for he promptly explained that the directorship he once shared in Dunfermline had now receded and gone into Bingo, so that he had no more business connections in the town, although he still operated the Kinema in Burntisland, and he added that a cinema manager had to be a jack-of-all-trades nowadays to survive, everything from stand-in projectionist to going round with the ice-lollies during the intervals. But here was I, who used to visit him on a bicycle, still working on the land, and now touring his vicinity with a motor car, which seemed a reflection of the times, with an emancipation of the farm worker and a decline in the cinema world in the face of television. Mr. Gilchrist was a very friendly and condescending man, and yet I used to stand and sweat with embarrassment in his panelled office, the smell of silage and cow dung still in my conscientious nostrils, while my body temperature, so long accustomed to the cold of the fields, found it hard to acclimatise with the suffocation of central heating.

Mr. Gilchrist remembered that I was something of a scribbler in my spare time and he was keenly interested when I told him of my progress in that direction. We talked on the value of the old cinema as an introduction to literature; even classical literature, as compared with the modern trend with its violence and sex, espionage and its woesome loss of story values, and that with all its gimmickry and technological advantages would never compensate for the golden days of its past maturity. Television was taking over in this department: what with the paperback version of the current T.V. saga on the bookshelves and the sound-track on long-play records the public were getting a fireside introduction to the classics in literature and music never previously available; something the cinema had pioneered and lost to the newer medium. Panoramic screen epics were a last ditch effort to entice the fans back to the stalls, but even in this belated experiment television was making an encroachment with their long-running period sagas, soon to be enhanced with colour by the studio boffins.

I remembered Mrs. Gilchrist from their courting days, but she carried on down the pavement, not knowing that an old acquaintance had hindered her husband, so we gabbled on like two geese in a farmyard, heedless of the traffic and the passing folk, and I introduced him to Jane, whom he had already met and still remembered as my wife from all those forgotten years. I asked Mr. Gilchrist if they had any children, and he said no, that he and his wife were still childless, when a passer-by hails him from the kerb and says his wife is waiting for him further down the street. But we spoke further about his father, who went under the stage name of George Hylands, whom I knew forty years ago in 1929, when he was manager of THE PICTURE HOUSE (Aubrey's) in Peterhead, before I met his son, who now tells me that his father died at 66 of a coronary attack after an operation for a prostrate gland. He also supplied me with cine literature, such as the old BIOSCOPE magazine from the silent days of the cinema.

So at last we shook hands, he with Jane also, and my friend made off, anxious to catch up with his wife, whom he said still had a full day ahead of her, whatever that might mean, as it was already mid-afternoon.

Leaving Dunfermline and lunching by the roadside I phoned Lorna from a public kiosk near Rumbling Bridge, mainly to enquire of her well-being, as she is expecting our first grandchild this coming week-end, and should be in hospital on

136

Saturday (16th). But she changes the subject and tells me my photo is in the Evening Express of Wednesday 13th, on the day we left home, and she says she is very pleased with my picture; that it is a "smashing photo", and the story that goes with it also very good. So I am somewhat elated with this and tells Jane in the car and we both wonder what the reporter has put in the article about my literary endeavours.

*Nearer Muthill we left the main road and drove down a farm track to look at the old chapel of Tullybardine, for I just can't resist these "ancient monuments", the aura of mystery and romance I associate with them, so I got the key to the chapel from the nearby farmhouse, and though it was late in the evening another couple came in after us and I left them with the key. Tullybardine was founded in 1446 by Sir Charles Murray, but is now devoid of pulpit or pews, just the bare stone and lime walls and the flagstone floor, and the living word of God has long been silent in this ancient lonely structure, where long ago the worshippers had come to hear it and to drink at the fountain of life. And thus by Crieff to Comrie, now almost asleep in its cradle of hills, and our tent just as we left it in the morning, and Mr. McGillivray going his last round of the site before bed-time.

August 15th, Friday

A brighter day, and the sun dappling the slopes with his golden fingertips, lifting the heart with gentle inspiration and filling the mind with the glories of creation.

We were up early, Jane and I, while the cushats were still crooning in the pinewoods; the rabbits hopping around the tents and caravans with their sleeping inhabitants. The smell of our bacon frying was strong in the air, attracting bee and wasp and midge to our tent door, so that we had to shut ourselves in with our plates on our knees. We were much refreshed from a good night's sleep and anxious to be on the road again.

Having filled the petrol tank we slipped quietly out of Comrie towards St. Fillans, where the waters lap the roadway and the yachts swing gently at their moorings. Further up the shores of Loch Earn the water was as smooth as a negative print, with the wooded hills photographed on its surface. Nearer Lochearnhead we stopped the car to watch the water-skiers, arcing the waters in ever widening circles of crystal spray, winding out and in among the red floating buoys at incredible speed, the motor-boat going round one side of the marker and the surf-rider round the other, cutting a figure 8 at each encirclement. One of the skiers was toppled into the loch in a splash of foam. The boat stopped to pick him up and soon he was on to his board again and off behind the tow-rope before you could take three drags on your fag.

At Lochearnhead we turned left and further on we made a diversion to Loch Voil and the Braes of Balquhidder, where we took pictures of Rob Roy's grave and the ruined chapel behind it, dating from 1331, and the graceful outline and belfry of the newer church nestling in the tree slopes. We inside this newer building, opening the creaking door in great curiosity, and the small empty church silent and lonely in the distant hills. Damp was affecting the plaster on the walls and there were several antiques dating from the Culdee and Celtic periods, besides a showcase bible printed in the Gaelic. The church is dedicated to Saint Angus, the patron saint of the parish of Balquhidder, and was built by David Carnegie of Stonvar around 1885. Leaving the church we walked up through the shady woods to the waterfall, which isn't very impressive, but beautiful in its secluded dell of sun-glanced leaves and moss-covered rocks, where the melody of the waters is like the harps of ancient minstrels.

After a glimpse at Loch Voil we back to the main road at King's House Inn and motored through Bonnie Strathyre, and often as I have heard and loved the song I never thought to look upon its setting:

"When the peak of Ben Vorlich is girdled with fire
And the evening falls gently on Bonnie Strathyre".

The late Neil Maclean sang it so beautifully on the Parlophone records with the plum-coloured label some 40 years ago, when it first caught my youthful ear. The lyrics were composed by author and poet Harold Boulton. I have also traced the source of its companion song "Bonnie Strathardle", and often as a youth have I sung them to myself to lighten my labours in the loneliness of the turnip fields, or among the stooks of the hairst park, where the lyrics filled my heart with a great nostalgia.

But now we motored into Callander and parked the car in a spacious square, where we had to pay for the privilege. Across the street was the Antler Garage and the Brown Trout restaurant, appropriately named for such a place. Here we did some shopping and wrote postcards and hunted for the post-office, tucked away at the far end of the main street, with another and smaller post-office at the opposite end, which I didn't discover until we left for Tannochbrae, and by then I had lost my patience and my temper.

Tannochbrae is the fictional township featured in the current television series of "Dr. Finlay's Casebook", from the stories of A. J. Cronin, and almost every visitor to Callander goes up the steep wooded hill to photograph Arden House, home of the worthy Dr. Cameron, played by Andrew Cruickshank, with actor Bill Simpson as his partner Finlay, and Barbara Mullen as Janet the housekeeper. But only the exteriors are filmed here and in reality Arden House is the private Auchingower Hotel. All the same we were determined not to be left out of the picture, having watched so much of it on the Telly at home.

We left the car a bit further up the hill and walked a mile-and-a-half to the Bracklin Falls. It says one mile on the signpost but it seemed the longest mile we ever walked and the road is impossible by car. But the spectacle of the falls is worth the journey, and long before you reach them you can hear the rushing boom of the waters deep in the wood. The water comes leaping down from the hills and slides over the Giant's Doorstep to darker depths in a head-swimming chasm with trees clinging to its rim. There is a frail footbridge over the centre of the falls, where the great rocks have been split by glacial or volcanic movement, standing on edge or lying at precipitous angles and forming ledges in the cavern, tearing the curtain of water to foaming shreds in its fall to the bottom. We crossed the bridge warily and crept along to the rim of the rock fissure, risking a glance at the spinning waters plunging into the whirlpool, but drawing back quickly with swimming heads.

Returning to Callander we went on to Doune Castle, where we cooked our dinner in the car park, mostly from tins on the stove, almost under the ramparts, and all the time we were tormented with bees and wasps from the honeysuckled walls of a nearby garden. The castle is magnificent and Jane took a picture of the river Teith from the highest coping on the turrets. The courtyard and walls were swarming with visitors and cameras were clicking from every angle of the battlements. At three bob a time for adults and half-price for the bairns, plus two-bob for a guidebook and a shilling for the car this castle viewing fiesta is becoming quite a lucrative sideline of the tourist industry. We walked round the broad curtain walls 40 feet from the ground and examined the great hall, the only part of the interior which seemed to be furnished, though restoration work might be in hand with the rest of the great building. It is from these forbidding walls at Doune Castle that we get the woesome lines of the old Scots ballad:

"Oh! lang will his lady
Look o'er the castle Doune
Ere she see the Earl O' Moray
Come sounding thro' the toon".

The lady's husband was the "Bonnie Earl o' Moray", murdered at Donibristle in Fife on February 7th, 1592, for his supposed courtship of Mary Queen of Scots. But in Scottish Balladry Lady Doune still sighs for her wayward husband.

Thence to Dunblane and its delightful cathedral, and if Dunfermline Abbey was transporting this was even more edifying:—This epic in stone, breath-catching in its whispered beauty; its interpretation of heavenly serenity, its scriptural association, its sublime architectural reverence, its angelic atmosphere of divine loveliness; its stone-kissed sanctity and sun-storied windows; its death-hushed aisles and incense-breathing charm, the floor-shaking throb of its mighty organ, the chime of its musical bells, its theme-thrown arches and shield-studded roof, a dedicated anthem of masonry to the glory of God. All hail Saint Blane and the story you have left us: this image in stone of a great creator; this saintly vision of a heaven on earth, where the rain is as soft as tears upon the chiselled stone.

Jane confided to me later that she prayed for Lorna in the small chapel within the cathedral.

I telephoned Lorna again from the kiosk at Gilmerton, and in the evening we drove through the Sma' Glen and lovely Glen Almond.

And so we come to the end of another short but delightful holiday, written here in memory's pages, to be enjoyed again in passing years of recollection—if we should by the Grace of God be spared so to do.

September 17th, Wednesday

Still on travel, but on a somewhat different scale, I would give you this question: If anyone asked you when the first parachute descent was made you would probably think for a moment or two and then you would come up with a date somewhere around the early or middle nineteen-twenties, or sometime during the later years of the First World War. Actually you would be about 172 years out, because the first descent by parachute from a balloon was accomplished in public and with exceptional courage by Andre Jacques Garnerin, a Frenchman, on October 22nd, 1797. And by the way a name like Garnerin isn't unlike Yuri Gagarin—the first man in space in our own century. Living as he did in the days of Napoleon I, Garnerin is also credited with the original idea of watching the movements of enemy troops from a balloon, but he was taken prisoner by the Austrians in 1793 before he had the opportunity of perfecting his idea. His balloon and parachute aeronautics were adventured after his release by the Austrians three years later in 1796. Even in our present adventurous century there seems little that is new under the sun. And wasn't it another Frenchman, Jules Verne, who first wrote of a journey to the moon, which has now been performed by the Americans.

September 27th, Saturday

Jane and I to the cinema, this time to the Majestic, in Union Street, Aberdeen, one of my favourite temples [demolished 1977], where I have seen some rare epics over the years. This time we were treated to an old scratched copy of THOSE MAGNIFICENT MEN IN THEIR FLYING MACHINES, which, despite its three years in the can had lost none of its sparkle. Flying scenes exhilarating and the machines an exact replica of the 1910 early flying period, including the strut-and-string machines and the flying bedstead. An excellent, almost all-star cast and the lovely Sarah Miles as sweet as your first ever cream-bun. Others contributing to the colourful anecdotal were Stuart Whitman, James Fox, Robert Morley, Gert Frobe, Terry Thomas, Eric Sykes and the late ill-fated Tony Hancock. And the film was produced by 20th Century Fox Film Corporation—in England I presume.

On the same programme, and from the same studio were Stan Laurel and Oliver Hardy in THE DANCING MASTERS, with Trudy Marshall, and directed by Malcolm St. Clair. Very funny and some good clowning from the stars, especially as the demonstrators of a dance routine at the start of the picture. A very young Robert Mitchum had a good part as the crook, looking every part the star he was to become in later years. A zany, good old-fashioned movie in black and white, now the exception in these days of colour. Admission 4/6d. each.

September 29th, Monday

I never expected to see the day when our old threshing mill would be dismantled and pulled out of the barn. But that is exactly what is happening here now and the barn is an empty shell. How long the mill has stood there in its cobwebs I couldn't say, but I have a suspicion that it had a predecessor with wooden cog-wheels for the driving belts, before the days of brass bushes and ball or roller bearings, away back in the days of the mill-course, revolving spars turned by horses to keep the mill going, something in the fashion of the French treadmill for the wine-presses, long before steam and the internal-combustion engine on the farms.

As this is a hill farm (Aikenshill) the old water-wheel as motivation is out of the question, and the windmill was never developed in Scotland to the extent that the Dutch have used it for industrial purposes, so we must assume from the shaft holes in the barn wall that horse-power was first employed here to drive the threshing mill. No doubt it was a vast improvement from the hand flail and enabled farmers to increase their corn acreage considerably with a smaller labour force, especially after the binders came in, though I am not sure which came first—the binders or the threshing mills, but I am inclined to think that their development was simultaneous.

Perhaps this would have been just over a hundred years ago, or about the middle of the nineteenth century, when steam was revolutionising industrial development. That there was a smoke stack and a stationary steam-engine at Aikenshill we have ample proof, because the water cistern for supplying the boiler is still extant, and the cinder grating still lies rusting in the stackyard; and if further conviction is needed you can see it in the square patch of blackened woodwork where the brick "lum" emerged from the slated roof of the engine "hoose".

Then came the oil-fired engine with its smaller exhaust and the smoke stack was demolished. The oil or paraffin engine lasted until half-through the present century, when electricity was wired to the farms and press-button threshing introduced, except at some places where the tractor pulley was employed for barn threshing. But electricity was late in coming to the farms and didn't last long as threshing power. Combine-harvesting was just round the corner and altered everything, the ultimate in factory farming and our old threshing mill now stands derelict in the farm close.

October 4th, Saturday

All the week with the cement mixer on the back of my tractor, laying an esplanade around the dairy door where there is always a sea of mud.

This week on the big screen at the Odeon, six rows from the front, at 4 shillings, I can almost pull the curtain aside or shake hands with the stars. Rod Steiger, Claire Bloom, Judy Geeson, Peggy Ashcroft and Paul Rogers in the Julian Blaustein production of Andrea Newman's novel, "3 INTO 2 WON'T GO". Directed by Peter Hall. Screenplay by Edna O'Brien. Photographed in colour on location in Surrey by Universal Pictures of America. A compelling domestic drama, outside the kitchen sink, but so realistic one feels he is playing Peeping Tom on the private affairs of an intimate household. Peggy Ashcroft and Claire Bloom particularly good as mother and daughter in trying circumstances. Oh why do people still insist upon real live theatrical performances? The Big Screen is even more intimate, more convincing, and the new celluloid copy will outlast flesh and bone. This can be resurrected when the theatre performance is only a memory.

On the same bill: Universal's EYE OF THE CAT, with Michael Sarrazin, Gayle Hunnicutt, Tim Henry and Eleanor Parker in a real clock forgetter, crammed with incident and eye-catching backgrounds; San Francisco in frazzling colours. And all the cats trained by Ray Berwick. The film directed by David Lowell Rich.

October 11th, Saturday

Well here I am back at the pictures again, and it's only a week since I was last time, and I've been doing this sort of thing for 40 years. A romantic you say! An idealist! A dreamer! —living in a fantasy world! Anyway, this is the last film review you will ever read in my diaries because I'm sick of writing them. And no wonder because somewhere among my papers there's a note or a cutting on almost every feature film I've ever seen, and I must have seen a few thousand in my time.

On this occasion it was two more of the "Carry On" comedies at the Grand Central, in George Street, Aberdeen. These were CARRY ON CLEO, a parody on Cleopatra, and a joyful nudge at the old Western in CARRY ON COWBOY. The cast list of both films were almost identical, except that in CLEO we had Amanda Barrie as the Egyptian Queen and Kenneth Connor as Caesar's bodyguard, while in COWBOY we had Bernard Bresslaw as the son of an Indian Chief, and Angela Douglas out from the big city to avenge the death of her father, a former sheriff in Podge City, out there in the cactus wastes, and she alighting from the red Wells Fargo stage like a veritable lily in the desert. Sidney James surprisingly good as the outlaw, and he also carried some weight (besides the armour) as Mark Antony. Warren Mitchell selling male slaves in the Roman markets. Sidney James good on the "draw", but

144

not fast enough for Jim Dale when the latter popped up from the manholes, taking pot shots at the outlaw on the High Street in Podge City. A very good and original gag. Others involved were Charles Hawtrey, Sheila Hancock, Joan Sims and Kenneth Williams. Director Gerald Thomas and produced by Peter Rogers at the Pinewood Studios for Warner-Pathe distribution. Old scratched copies but the colours still fast and captivating. A lot of people in the cinema as this series is very popular and making a lot of money, many times over the cost of production.

November 1st, Saturday

Once more winter is upon us down on the farm. And you can't travel far from here in winter because the day is too short, and the only alternative in the dark nights is the movies, which isn't all that difficult when Aberdeen and the bright lights is only ten miles distant. And I did promise I wouldn't ever write another film review but here I am again, a born critic in the wrong calling, but this is definitely my last fling at dramatic appraisal.

This time I left Jane at home with the kitchen sink, and I alone to the Regal A.B.C., where they were screening Clive Donner's ALFRED THE GREAT! starring David Hemmings, Prunella Ransome and Michael York. Ransome by the way is a name we farming folk have always associated with the best in agricultural implements, made by the firm of Ransomes Sims & Jeffries Ltd., of Ipswich I believe, and I just wonder where Miss Prunella fits in here, and whether she is a relation of the founder, having such an uncommon name, unless we use it as that other noun without the (e) at the end, which puts a different colour on it altogether.

But here I digress from the battle scenes between the Saxons and the Danes, which were very good, but the dramatics of the piece somewhat amateurish and unconvincing, not to be compared with Peter O'Toole's portrayal of Henry II in THE LION IN WINTER. But here again the "Lion" was caged and the action limited, whereas with ALFRED's battles and O'Toole's acting ability I think we would have had an excellent combination, realistic and colourful. The stake Palisades used by the

145

Saxons to deflect the Danish spears was most authentic, something we have used in the sheepfold and to break snowdrifts, which was maybe how Alfred got the idea. But I didn't like David Hemmings as Alfred, nor Miss Ransome as his Queen. His face lacks expression, almost boyish if not effeminate, and Miss Ransome is all freckles, almost a nettle rash, though her eyes are pleasant, and I felt that the whole thing (apart from the fighting) was rather like a concert in the local school hall.

November 22nd, Saturday

I am off the leash again, this time to a show of slides on railway lore by the Railway Preservation Society in the Y.M.C.A. Hall in the city. Steam locomotives, derelict stations, dilapidated coaches and rolling stock, a colourful demonstration, followed by tea and the sale of postcards. Twenty-eight enthusiasts attended and three of them I recognised and talked with from a film show last night in Robert Gordon's College. There was a whip-round to defray expenses so I put a shilling in the plate and bought two postcards of old railway engines in stunning colours, things I used to collect in my boyhood, before any of my companions here were born, in the great days of steam.

I afterwards to an arts and crafts exhibition in the old Music Hall in Union Street, where almost every recreational club in the city was represented, excepting the Writers' Circle and the Amateur Cinematograph Society. But most of the others were there, including the Aberdeen Aero Club, the Yachting Club, the Radio Hams, the Camera Club, Allotment Holders, Ski Club, etc., Girl Guides, Red Cross, Army Cadets, Highland dancing, piping, fiddling, fencing, sculpture, painting, Library Service, etc., etc. But the highlight for me was a show of 16 mm films and coloured transparencies with guitar music and commentary on tape by members of the Aberdeen Camera Club. It was an artistic choice of subject on wild life and the commentary elegantly spoken—beautifully done, entrancing show. You see I am tremendously interested in other people's hobbies: how they occupy their spare time, what they do and why they do it.

146

November 30th, Sunday

Jane and I to Sunnyside, Kingswells, to see Jackie, our number 2 son and his wife Lorna, and little Linda Jane, who is now three months old and thriving every day. I do believe she is a bit like her old grandad, yours truly, and a lot of people agree.

December 25th, Thursday

Birth of our first grandson, Martin James Reid, a 7 lb. Christmas boy child, born at 10.13 this morning at Foresterhill Hospital to Beryl Anne Stott and our Graham (Rupert in my former journals). I had resolved to keep my diary open for this event but now hereafter I shall close it, except to record our holidays. This boy may keep our name alive, but never in any of our families has there ever been a Martin; it is a fine sounding name and well chosen, and the James is after the two great-grandfathers on our side, Jane's father, who is still alive, and my own father, James Gray Reid, who died 20 years ago. God bless his stainless soul for ever and ever, Amen.

1970

August 7th, Friday

After a whirlwind courtship of only two months, our oldest
son, Eric Douglas, who is 34, and on a three months spree from
Malaysia, was married at Foveran Church today at 4 p.m. by
the Rev. T. J. Dyer, to Miss Ann Strachan 25, photographer's
receptionist, and elder daughter of Mr. Alex. M. Strachan,
insurance surveyor, and Mrs. Strachan, 23 Countesswells
Avenue, Aberdeen.

Reception afterwards at the Craighall Inn, Ellon, where we
were regaled with high-class cuisine and witty speeches and we
toasted the bridal pair in sparkling champagne. A colourful,
happy, sociable evening and everyone present seemed to enjoy
themselves immensely. We took the opportunity of having
our family picture taken in a coloured group, Jane and
myself seated on chairs in front, and our three sons with their
wives standing behind. Ann, our latest daughter-in-law, tall,
dark and slim, still in her white, flowing dress, Lorna with
Jackie and Beryl with Graham. Graham was Best Man to
his brother and the bridesmaid was 24-year-old Miss Margery
Collins of Aberdeen, a cousin to Ann. Eric and Jackie
both have beards nowadays and they come out well in the
photographs.

The families on both sides mixed and danced tremendously
well and this time I suspect that the Willoxes met their match
in the Strachans for sociability, dancing and drinking generosity. There were only four people there on my side, including
my sister and her man from Stonehaven. The Reids were in a
minority, but what with our two grandchildren, Linda and
Martin, and Lorna expecting her second child, our family
is enlarging; expanding from my grandmother who gave
her maiden name to her illegitimate child who became my
father.

Missing from the wedding was the Grand Old Man of the
Willox family, Jane's father, who is 82, and meantime in
hospital with an appendicitis.

August 17th, Monday

Eric and Ann left Dyce airport at 7.45 this morning for Glasgow and Amsterdam, where they are to spend a few days (Eric on business contacts) and thus on to Bangkok and Kuala Lumpur, arriving there around Friday or Saturday morning.

In the evening Jane and I to see the Andy Stewart Show at His Majesty's Theatre in Aberdeen.

August 19th, Wednesday

Motored to Comrie, in Perthshire, where we pitched camp at West Lodge Caravan Site, for a few days holiday, in the same place we were last year.

August 20th, Thursday

Visited Scone Palace, which has been long on my waiting list, and we walked among Jacob's Lambs in the park. Spent about an hour in the palace, then outside to the rain. Later to Perth, where it was still raining, so we inside the museum and art galleries, also Fair Maid's House. I then to St. Ninian's Episcopal Cathedral Church, on the corner of Atholl Street and Methven Street, but the interior was mounted to the roof in high scaffolding, where workmen were scrambling about like busy spiders on a web, rewiring the building. Wood carving of the saints very beautiful in fretwork, and I stood admiring them a long time in the dim light, transported almost in my admiration of the artist, my soul elevated and restful in the silent majesty of the great building, darkened almost to twilight while the workmen talked and joked on the high rafters. The minister came in from a side door, a long figure in black and a white collar and his hands behind his back. We talked for a while and he apologised for the uproar the church was in because of the renovations, and he asked where I came from and I told him of my abiding love for churches, whereupon he said I could stay as long as I liked, but as Jane was waiting in the car I didn't stay much longer, but outside to the rain.

On the way back to Crieff we struck off on a side road on the left to the old kirk at Wester Fowlis, where we opened the creaking door and tip-toed around the empty pews in the silent dusk. Outside the rain had ceased and the smoke rose straight from the village chimneys, while we wandered on the wet grass among the old leaning gravestones.

August 21st, Friday

Raining again, so we motored to Innerpeffray Library, near Crieff, the oldest Free Library in Scotland. Some very old prints here that fully absorbed my interests and many famous celebrities have visited the library over the centuries. We then motored to Monzie Kirk, where it was still raining, and two workmen in oilskin suits were scything the long grass in the churchyard. We sat in the car a while, not knowing where to go, but eventually the sun came out and cleared the skies, so we motored through Glen Almond and the Sma' Glen to Dunkeld and Pitlochry, where we took some colour photographs of the picture book village of Moulin, then doubled back to Aberfeldy, Killin, Lochearnhead, St. Fillans and Comrie. Today hardly worth recording, except that we had a glimpse of Taymouth Castle, that fretwork of stone in symmetrical majesty, the architect's dream of perfection.

August 22nd, Saturday

Still raining. Motored down from Comrie to Falkland, in the Kingdom of Fife, where we went on a conducted tour of the old Royal Palace of the Stuarts. Historical building in classical architecture and the chapel very impressive in its silent beauty. We walked round an exhibition of paintings in the Town Hall. Most original work by local artists, chief among them being a Miss Julia Wilson for her work with paint and sea-shells in floral design, and J. H. Williams for his delightful landscapes. We also went into the Parish Church in Falkland, a Gothic building of great size and the outer walls heavily buttressed, supporting an enormous spire which dwarfs the town and its old houses with thatched and red-pantiled roofs. These houses, known I believe as "Fife Harling", are gradually being restored to their original design by the National Trust, carefully preserving the quaint character of this Neuk of Fife.

August 23rd, Sunday

The rain has ceased at last and the day is lovely. Motored via Lochearnhead to Glen Ogle, where I stopped to photograph the old railway viaduct which used to carry the line from Perth to Crianlarich, a picturesque sight at the foot of the mountain, but still 300 feet above the level, and a tiny mountain stream trickles through one of the giant arches. Thence to Crianlarich and Tyndrum and down Loch Awe, where Jane snapped my picture against a backdrop of Kilchurn Castle and Ben Cruachan. I picked out three more castles on the islands of the loch, which I took to be Froach, Innes Channel and Furn-chairn, in that order, the last a very picturesque and romantic ruin close at the water's edge, but we forgot to take the camera out of the car and couldn't be bothered to scramble back for it. We got out again at Kilmartin and walked around the great assembly of carved stones in the churchyard. Then on to Lochgilphead, Inveraray (where we had to queue for fish and chips) then through the mountains to Arrochar, in the shadow of the Cobbler, and back to Crianlarich.

August 24th, Monday

On our way home we made a diversion to Blair Castle, where we examined everything in the 32 rooms open to the public, and I was greatly taken with the expansive array of coloured miniatures, little gems in the Gainsborough fashion which held me greatly enthralled. And thus home to Aikenshill before nightfall.

1973

It is now almost three years since I wrote a scrap in my travel diary, though in the intervening period I have been busy editing the former entries and hammering them into shape for public scrutiny—or at least that was my intention, though one never knows with these things.

Also in that interlude I have endured a shattering nervous breakdown, even worse than my last one of nearly 20 years ago. On that occasion I spent two months in a mental hospital, as I have written elsewhere, and underwent electrical shock treatment to try and shake off my depression, with some creditable success. This latest attack was so intense and sudden that I was completely overwhelmed and spent some six weeks in the Ross Clinic in Aberdeen, where I was put under sedation, but managed to recover gradually without shock treatment, because this time I knew from experience that it wasn't the cure for my present malady. Only time and recrimination with myself could sort that out. For therapy I corrected the proof sheets for my first published book HARD SHINING CORN, the most humiliating defeat of my life and my greatest triumph coinciding in the same day, the publisher, Mr. Paul Harris, delivering my manuscript personally on the morning I went into hospital. So let it be known that I corrected the proofs of that book with the tears running down my cheeks, a book that has since brought joy and pleasure to thousands, or so I have reason to believe, and one man it actually cured of sickness, reading it in bed until he forgot he was ill and was soon quite well again. But of course we don't know what his ailment was and it may not have been a serious one; but psychologically at least the book may have lightened the tedium and hastened recovery.

For me it was a heart-breaking experience, running over my beloved lines with tears in my eyes; my day of elation turned to one of despair, with all I had hoped and prayed for in ruins, reduced almost to imbecility of mind among strangers, where Jane's comforting hand was of little avail in my distress of soul. It has been written that genius can kill and now I believe it.

Not that I consider myself a genius, but that the genie within me had turned my pen into a knife thrusting at my own heart, destroying my will to live, so that I couldn't trust my own hands, lest I should strangle myself. Genius you say! I had barely glanced at the ethereal gold when it withered my soul to ashes, leaving me to crawl in the dust. A little learning is indeed a dangerous thing, and I had filled myself drunk with knowledge. I had torn the veil of reason that divides us from insanity, and in a drugged sleep I had to patch up the crack again. It was a traumatic experience. Beyond the veil was chaos and I reeled back from the bottomless pit. I could not bear to look upon it and survive, and choking with fear I fought my way back; back to God's world and sanity.

Even yet, two years after the attack, I am still writing with a sick mind, striving to regain a balanced equilibrium. The same qualities of mind that give me such flashing glimpses of elysium can also open the gates of hell for me. To quote from my own poem "Frustration":

And mark my wing-singed search for ethereal fire,
Searching the Infinite:
Feeling and seeing where few have touched
The dew made molten gold at the sun's forge.

Of this I must be wary in future, and never to trust fickle fortune; least of all when she smiles over me with her gifts, for as Cowper says she is blind and sees not what she gives to human mortals.

I would never have believed (nor could I foresee) that my departure from the country to the city would bring me such bitterness of heart. Mechanisation in the country was killing me anyway; making a rat race of what I had formerly known as a pleasant environment, and I sought refuge in the city. But the city of my dreams turned to nightmares, spreading her snares for my unwary feet. I had lived long enough to know that the grass isn't any greener on the other side of the fence, even though it looks so; and I knew that all that glitters isn't gold—I even looked before I leaped, but even so, I was no match for fate and what she had in store for me. I thought I was clever but I was no match for destiny. Yet a second and third time in my life I have been unmanned and humbled,

153

brought to the dust from on high by the Almighty, perhaps as a punishment for trespassing on the higher spheres, or that the light of His countenance was too strong for my feeble eyes.

It never rains but it pours as they say, for in the midst of my mental distress Jane's father died, quietly and suddenly at the age of 83 on November 15th, 1971, while I was still in hospital. On a day of cold driving sleet I stood shivering at his graveside and saw him lowered to his last resting place. I was a nervous wreck, afraid that one of my delusions would hit me, stunning me almost with its intensity, bringing my heart into my throat with fear, pounding at my rib cage and throbbing the blood throughout my body, raising the pressure to bursting point, until with sheer will power I soothed it into calm. But I was calm on that funeral day, concerned for Jane at the passing of her father, and I stood by her at the last bugle call. So there goes James Willox, one of the greatest Scottish characters of the old school of farm workers I have ever known, who could tell stories by the dozen, some of them humorous and some of them sad; the man who, 30 years ago took his holidays to nurse me back to health after double pneumonia, strengthening me day by day with teaspoonfuls of rum—the man who saved my life on that drastic occasion.

So here I am at 60, white and shaken, my hair grey and wind-blown, standing on the battlefield of Sheriffmuir, fulfilling a boyhood aspiration in spite of all my troubles. And whoever writes my biography (if anyone thinks I deserve one) don't let him strew my path with rose petals, rather with thorns and briars, with perhaps an occasional blossom by the wayside; for my road through life has not been easy, nor my footing smooth, and but for my extraordinary constitutional strength I would not have survived to tell the tale.

I have left Jane in the car, preferring to look over the knick-knacks she had bought to take home. This was another of these daft pilgrimages to the shrines of my boyhood, read from my history books at school, that only late in life I have had the opportunity to fulfil. So I left Jane in our Viva and walked a mile from the monument on the road through the Ochil Hills to the battlefield of Sheriffmuir. The gathering stone of the clans is protected by an iron grille cemented into the ground, consisting of three boulders set together to hold the Jacobite flagstaff, and the stones still bear the marks where the Highlanders whetted their dirks before the battle.

A ladder chained to a tree enables the visitor to ascend to a platform where he can survey the moor, at this time of year sprinkled with heather bells so rich in colour they look like drops of blood. Of these I gathered a handful and some marsh cotton, besides a small blue star flower to preserve in my book of memories.

The battle was fought on a Sunday, the thirteenth of November, 1715, between the Earl of Mar with his Highlanders, and the Duke of Argyll in command of the Royalist army. Both commanders arranged their forces out of sight of the other, the westward ridge of the Ochils between them, so that when the combatants met in conflict each outflanked the other, causing great confusion, and giving rise to the old song which says:

> "There's some say that we wan,
> And some say that they wan,
> And some say that nane wan at a', man;
> But one thing I'm sure,
> That at Sherramuir,
> A battle there was, that I saw, man.
> And we ran and they ran,
> And they ran and we ran,
> And we ran and they ran awa', man".

The Wappenshaw of Sheriffmuir lies about two miles above Dunblane on the Ochil Foothills, where the sheriffs of those days trained the local youths in musketry.

Rob Roy and about 500 of his kilted followers watched the running battle from a safe distance, and later robbed the dead. Horse and foot soldiers were employed on both sides but the result was inconclusive. Nevertheless, it prevented the Highlanders from joining the English Jacobite forces, who were defeated at Preston, and thus ended the Rebellion for the Old Pretender, father of Prince Charlie, who tried again, with bitter results for the Stuarts in 1745.

The monument by the roadside is to the Clan Macrae and inscribed thus: "In memory of the Macraes killed at Sheriffmuir 13th November, 1715 when defending the Royal House of Stuart. The Kintail and Lochalsh companies formed part of the left wing of the Highland army and fell almost to a man"— Erected at the instance of the Clan Macrae Society, 13th November, 1915.

The inscription is also given in Gaelic.

We were in a caravan on the Arnbro site at Crieff, that beautiful town in its valley of hills, like a fair lady asleep among flowers. On the previous day, Wednesday, July 4th we went by train from Gleneagles to Edinburgh, where Jane and I had a look at my manuscript Diaries in the National Library, and we met custodian Mr. James Ritchie, who treated us with great cordiality.

We also visited the Safari Park at Drummond Castle, near Stirling, where we photographed some of the animals, while a monkey sat on the bonnet of our car. Lions lay on the grass, mostly in groups, seemingly asleep, except for the occasional whisk of a tail against the flies. There were leopards, two young elephants, two antelopes, several zebras and giraffes, all at large and all quite willing to have their pictures taken, though visitors were warned to stay in their cars and to keep the windows closed. A tremendous attraction for the children was a dolphin display in a fibre-glass tank within the grounds of the castle.

I walked on the old railway viaduct which spans the valley at Lochearnhead, which used to carry the railway to Crieff. These old bridges fascinate me and this one is of tremendous height and length considering the small stream which runs underneath one of the giant arches. It is similar to the one in Glen Ogle, on the same line, which I photographed three years ago.

My book, HARD SHINING CORN is in the library at Crieff.

1974

August 31st, Friday

Well, well, here I am again, and it is over a year since I wrote a single word in my diary—when we were on holiday last year at Crieff. This year we chose Clydebank, the Cloch caravan site at Gourock, overlooking the Cloch Lighthouse on the Firth of Clyde. We stayed a week here, motoring round the area and taking the train to Glasgow. The huge end window on the caravan gave us a panoramic view of the Firth, stretching to Dunoon on the opposite shore, Holy Loch, Kilcreggan and the Gairloch. After dark the far shore twinkled with lights, and at dusk, while the mountains were still visible, it was as if they had put on their necklaces of sparkling jewellery that reflected on the water. It is a twilight spectacle I would compare with Kessock on the Beauly Firth, with the massive shoulder of Ben Wyvis lowering in the distance. Here on the Clyde the great ships throbbed past our window, their engines vibrating the hill on which our caravan was perched. Through the trees one evening, with binoculars, we watched a huge Polaris submarine emerge from Holy Loch, submerged almost to the conning tower and the high fish tail, like that of a whale, leaving a wide white arc on the dark water, a black sinister monster with the fate of the world in its hidden fists.

During the day we sometimes sat in the car on Gourock pier and watched the numerous ferry-boats chugging idly at their moorings, loading passengers and cars for trips round the islands and to places like Dunoon and Rothesay and several others on the Argyle coast. Hundreds of yachts bobbed and swung on their coloured buoys, while the swell from a passing ship increased their motion.

Largs is a most delightful place, to my mind surpassing even Ayr or Oban for scenic loveliness converging on the ocean. Such tall and graceful spires on the blue water's edge, the white buildings sweeping back to the green and purple hills, so restful to the eye, where the mind may linger on their memoried slopes, reaching to the blue sky with its white cloud patterns. South of the town, between the railway and the sea, stands the "Pencil" of Largs, the pseudo-Pictish monument built to commemorate the Battle of Largs in 1263, fought between the Vikings of Norway, under King Haco, and the Scottish army led by Alexander III, in which the Norsemen were repulsed with great slaughter. There was a striking picture of the battle in my school history book, the Scots and Vikings hacking at each other in close quarters, swords and axes waving on high, with the high-prowed Longships in the background, driven from Arran by a stormy wind, forcing the Vikings to try their luck at Largs. The battle was so decisive in favour of the Scots I believe that it was the last attempted landing in Scotland by the wild men of Scandinavia. I read about the battle when I was 12; 50 years later I stand upon the seaweed where it was fought 700 years ago.

Motoring up from Dalry to Johnstone I went out of my way to look at the Wallace monument at Elderslie, where the great warrior was born. Here I learned that he was imprisoned after his capture by the traitor Menteith at Dumbarton Castle, nestling between the twin summits on that huge rock, Dumbarton Rock, dominating the Clyde at the mouth of the river Leven. The rock is 240 feet high and is rivalled by another cleft-rock on the shore near Dumbuck, where quarrying by excavators is meantime in progress.

Erskine Ferry is now a huge modern bridge of steel and concrete over the Clyde, high enough to take the largest ships and rivalling the Forth Road Bridge in majesty, straddling the river with its huge legs in the water. We crossed the bridge to Helensburgh from the Greenock side, again on the road back, and on the way home, paying 15p. each time in toll fees. I missed the bridge going down, when I took the wrong turning at Stirling; in fact I didn't turn at all but held straight on the M9 and the M80 to Glasgow. This was something I had dreaded doing, especially when I landed on a six-lane highway, but being a Sunday I was spared the heavier traffic and the roads were sign-posted overhead, which I think is a good idea if there was snow on the roadway, obliterating the road numbers.

Clydeside was completely new to us and far more beautiful than I had ever imagined, despite the huge ship-building yards and the industrial belt. It wasn't till later I learned that

Burns' Highland Mary is buried at Greenock, near the old West Kirk, and I believe she died of typhoid. What with all the convulsion of modern road-making and redevelopment some of these ancient shrines may be sacrificed or removed to other places, though I hope not.

Motoring towards Helensburgh, from Dumbarton, we passed through Cardross, and although the name seemed to ring a bell in my memory the place appeared to be of little interest. We merely stopped to mail a few postcards and I discovered that King Robert Bruce died in the castle here on June 7th, 1329, fifteen years after Bannockburn, and they must have carried his body from here to Dunfermline, his heart to Melrose, on its return from the Holy Land. The castle is three miles from the little town but we could find no trace of it.

From Garelochhead we returned to Helensburgh, as well named as beautiful, where we stopped for tea on the promenade, among hundreds of other cars and a multitude of shoppers and sightseers. A plinth on the seafront commemorates the pioneering spirit of Henry Bell, designer of the Comet Steamship, and the flywheel of the famous vessel is preserved in Hermitage Park. From here we crossed to Balloch and Bonhill, where I was delighted to find myself in the neighbourhood of Tobias Smollett, eighteenth-century novelist, who describes the Vale of Leven so beautifully in verse:

> Pure stream, in whose transparent wave
> My youthful limbs I used to lave,
> No torrent stains thy limpid source,
> No rocks impede thy dimpling course,
> That sweetly warbles o'er its bed
> With white round polished pebbles spread.

Not unlike poor Peter Still on my own "dimpling" Ugie. Ironically, the day we went to Bonhill two youths of 18 from Dumbarton were drowned while bathing in the Leven, which I suppose is the overflow from Loch Lomond into the Clyde at Dumbarton. Smollett was born near Bonhill House, an old seat of the Smollett family in 1721. Returning over the Erskine Bridge I took a wrong turning again and landed on the motorway to Paisley, on the suburbs of Glasgow. I was so thankful when I found a parking space in Paisley and a passing workman managed to direct me back on to the motorway where I could find a branch to Greenock. We had delightful fish and chips at Gourock and a look at the ferries and the railway station before returning to Cloch and its quaint old lighthouse.

Next day we headed south, through Inverkip and Hunterston (where some new power installation is in progress) and along the beach at Wemyss Bay, where the Peaks of Arran followed us on the skyline, friendly but aloof across the hazy firth. At West Kilbride we bought the most delightful apple-tart and home-made pies which we later had for tea in a layby. Meanwhile we motored up the steep hill for a closer look at the majestic ruin of Law Castle, close by a farm on the top of the brae. On asking the name of the castle of two women in the town one of them smiled and asked if I wanted to buy it? Perhaps she thought I was an oil magnate or a rich tourist looking for an ancestral home? But I smiled back with my hands in my pockets and said no, though I might take a photograph of the place—which I didn't after all, though it was quite impressive at close quarters. Here as elsewhere in these regions the railway stations invite me: still reminiscent of old-time traditional railway respectability; flowers, posters, waiting-room and ticking clock, bridge over the track and a porter on the platform. Despite Jane's impatience (we merely wanted the toilets) I had her wait until the train from Largs came in, dropping its passengers and picking one up, then gliding on its way to Glasgow.

I turned left at Kilwinning, stopping on a hill overlooking Stevenston, where I could sweep my binoculars from Saltcoats to Kilmarnock, and all that lay between on the Ayrshire coast, with Lady Isle in focus, offshore from Troon. Saltcoats is a name that intrigues me; I don't know why and I cannot imagine its origin. Overlooking Irvine I discerned another literary association in the fact that John Galt, author of "Annals of the Parish", was born here in 1779 (died 1839). Also born here James Montgomery the poet (1772-1854).

Flickering in my glasses was the old castle of Dundonald, secluded on a grassy bank inward from the coast and surrounded by new townships and factories; the very old still surviving in the midst of nuclear twentieth-century commotion and upheaval. King Robert II died here in 1390, Dundonald being a seat of the Royal Stuarts. In this area lived also the beautiful Susanna, Countess of Eglinton, to whom Allan Ramsay dedicated his GENTLE SHEPHERD. She died in Auchans House in 1780 in her 91st year. So much for enduring beauty.

We went to Glasgow twice by train, first from Gourock by electric train, and two days later from Largs by diesel unit. I wanted a seat behind the driver on the front coach, which was exhilarating at first, swinging along the Largs coast, until we reached a long dark tunnel approaching Fort Matilda station, when the clatter and noise was like all hell let loose about our ears, unnerving and fearful to anyone unaccustomed to the journey. On the bends nearer Paisley Junction the speed and swing of the rocking carriage was even more terrifying, and Jane said it served me right for wanting to sit at the front of the train, that I could have stayed further back and I wouldn't have seen so much. But Jane was scared also, and clutching my sleeve; the coach seemed so wide and the rails so narrow you thought it couldn't possibly keep on the track, like a horse cart running on knitting needles as my wife remarked, and must surely collide with oncoming monsters on the other track to Dalry. But we knew that trains ran here every day and we never heard of accidents. And our driver seemed relaxed and unworried, with one hand on the brake while he rolled a cigarette with the other, quietly observing the litter that had been thrown on the line from the bridges: sticks, stones, tins and grocers' cartons, and I no longer envied his job as a train driver. Then it suddenly dawned on me that our driver had other things to worry about besides the swing of the train, for this was the notorious railway into Glasgow where the kids make sport of throwing stones from the bridges at the train drivers. I remembered reading in the papers recently of the train driver who was killed when an overhanging electric cable carrier came through his windscreen, broken by a huge boulder from a bridge. Under one such bridge I observed an iron wheel-barrow carelessly up-ended at the side of the rails. It may have been a workman's barrow, but what if one of those vandal youths should set it on the rails, and the thought appalled me. But our driver seemed unperturbed as he ploughed through the rubbish, paper bags and newspapers flying in all directions, and where new track was laid he slowed down to a crawl, the train tip-toeing over the new rail joints, which further raised our respect for him, and I noticed that with every green signal light we approached a bell rang in his cabin. He went gliding into Glasgow Central in quiet gracefulness, with a timely "Honk-honk" on the horn to a shunter who was coming a bit too close to the main line; now clicking over the selected points to the desired platform, slow and careful to the approaching red buffers at the terminus, which we now regarded as a pier of refuge from tumultuous seas.

Returning home we took an Ayr express, pulled by a diesel locomotive, and we had a seat in the middle of the train, far behind the drivers and their lurching monster, where the journey was fast and smooth and comfortable; where all fear was forgotten in the flashing past of pleasant sunny countryside, consoled in the rhythm of metal wheels on the rail joints, relaxing in the swoosh of bridges and the small stations we left behind. We shared the compartment with three long-haired youths drinking beer out of cans, no doubt regarding Jane and myself as two old fogeys, for they were young enough to be our grandsons almost. We were apprehensive for a time in their company, not that we minded them drinking beer out of cans, for our own sons do the same thing, but we had heard so many stories of these type of youths taking advantage of older people; but then we realised they had been working all the week in Glasgow, for it was Friday night, and they were on their way back to Ayr and their folks for the week-end. One of them even gave me a cigarette and a light and they looked at Jane as a sort of mother figure deserving their utmost respect. As we had to change for Largs at Dalry, and I didn't know the stations, the youths gave me some warning on the approach of the junction, when the train slowed down and we got out on the platform. The Largs train was waiting, a diesel unit again, and once aboard we soon reached about 60 miles-an-hour without concern, swinging through the forests in a wide sweep to the sea-shore at Fairley High station, the trees like shimmering screens of green at the windows, then through the noisy tunnel where the devil was still at his hammering, and along the coast to Largs, where the tide was out and beachcombers were looking for sea-shells in the evening sun.

But we were impressed with Glasgow, especially with its allocation of traffic in motorcades and fly-overs and the shopping precincts reserved strictly for pedestrians. For once the shopping arcades intrigued me more than Kelvingrove, probably because I am weary of museums and exhibitions and all their musty treasures, though I enjoyed some of my favourite busts in the galleries, like Tolstoy, Carlyle, Shaw and Ruskin, and of the old masters I preferred the English painters to what we saw of Dutch, French or Italian, though the latter were best when inspired by the religious theme. There is a certain gloominess over Continental painting which is not observed in English work; here the colours are brighter and the subject better defined, or should I say illuminated, less obscured in cloud and cloak of mythology; but then perhaps my lack of experience may be to blame for not discerning the better judgement in classical art. But there you have the opinion of a layman.

I am now in my sixty-second year and Jane will be 58 on September 10th. We have been together since our youth (Jane was nearing 17 when we met and I was nearing 20) and now we are growing old together in a new age of punch-ticket travel, self-help shops and restaurants and robot service. Yet I think we have adapted ourselves very well to the change in our living habits, though the penny is slow to drop sometimes and we find ourselves in the most awkward situations, though the people of Glasgow were most helpful and courteous when we went wrong. There was the time when we came away from the serving counters with two dinners on one tray, and without knives and forks, until another customer told us where to find them without having to go to the end of the queue again. But the railway porter was less obliging when I put both our tickets in the turnstile and it wouldn't open to let us through. We had to ring for the aid of a surly porter who came with a key to let us out, like cattle from a pen. He was even more disgruntled when I misread 18.35 hours on the platform departure board for 8.35 p.m. I should have understood it was 6.35 p.m. but I can never understand this twice round the clock method of reading the time and I always get lost after twelve hours. We were never taught to read the hours in teens and always went back to one o'clock instead of saying 13 hours and so many minutes. But the porter at the platform gate made no allowances for us and was full of sarcasm when we thought we had missed our train.

But I liked the bustle of Glasgow railway station though I can never make out what the announcer is saying over the loudspeaker. And despite the discourtesy of some of the staff (which I think has replaced some of the discipline and respect of the older generation of railway workers)—despite this, and the fact that I had to pay twopence for a pee in Glasgow Central, which once was free—I still hanker for the railways. I even admire their endeavour and thankless efforts to survive in this era of motorcades and air travel that would wipe them from the slate of recorded industrial progress. And when I say survive you only have to glance at all those deserted stations and empty goods yards and nettle-grown tracks to realise the truth of it, or to what degradation the railways have sunk from their former glories.

On the day we motored down to Largs I made another blunder. The car park barrier was down against entry but there was plenty of space inside. I was surprised at this and motored past it twice to make sure. Car Park was clearly printed at the entrance and "Full" was underneath, but not illuminated, and that was what tricked me. I should have understood it would have been lit up if the park was full, but I didn't and read it synonymously with "Car Park". We motored around somewhat perplexed, looking for parking space on the streets, which was impossible, even in the morning, and we wondered why the authorities wouldn't let us into the public car park, thinking maybe it was a local show day and that they were reserving the space for special guests, especially when we had seen some kilted Highlanders walking the pavements, like the members of a pipe band. Then we noticed a car approach the barrier and up it went automatically and in popped the car, like something I've seen only in a Laurel and Hardy movie. But being as stupid as Stan and Ollie anyway maybe we could try it too, though not too fast in case it didn't work and the pair of us might end up on our backsides with a tyre round our necks. So I looked to see if the coast was clear and made a U-turn on the High Street, then had a tilt at the boom with the Viva, like an armoured knight at a jousting tournament.

But sure enough, up went the boom without a human being near it and in we sailed, though heaven knows what would happen if you were at speed, never giving the robot time to notice you, though he might be faster than you think if you tried him out.

A man with a money bag strapped to his shoulder directed me to a vacant space, and after parking and locking the car doors I went over and offered to pay him. It was 15 pence he said and pay when you go out. I walked over to the exit with Jane and put 10 pence in the meter, and I was about to insert the other 5p. when the man came after me and asked what I was doing. I said you told us to pay when we left and I put 10p. in the slot machine. He unlocked the box and gave me back my 10p., informing us it was for the car to get out, not us alone. We must wait until we took the car out, then we could pay and the barrier would rise, otherwise someone else would take the immediate advantage of an open gate. Such fools we were but we're wiser now.

In Glasgow I was foolish enough to ask a policeman on duty if he knew so-and-so, who had joined the force there some years ago. There was this police sergeant with three stripes on his arms standing in the Trongate, the traffic and pedestrians flowing on all sides, yet he looked at me kindly and said there were twenty-five hundred policemen in Glasgow and that they needed them all in a place like this. No he didn't know so-and-so and if I knew what was good for me maybe I shouldn't go further up the Trongate at this hour when the pubs were just closing, with some ruffians on the street, and he directed me back to the arches of the Central Station, where we might be safer. I had less success with this bobby than the Irishman had with his London equivalent. At any rate the traffic never stopped and I had no song like "The Mountains o' Mourne" to regale him with.

I couldn't conclude my holidays without a mention of the cinema; that other passion in my life which has been with me since my childhood, colouring the events in my episodic existence like a picture calendar, claiming my adulation almost to the extent that some men would lavish on a woman. Except in the centre of the big cities the cinemas everywhere are in a sorry state. Mostly gone over to Bingo or closed for

165

good, their doors and windows shuttered up with boards to protect them from vandals. Those that survive are showing mostly sex nightmares or monster science fiction horror epics, or as one critic puts it: "Spaghetti western with plenty of ketchup thrown in". The stills are reminiscent of the silent era, when action was predominant, but was good clean fun on train roofs and there was no spilling of blood at the bridges. Now the posters are even bloodstained and the action is violence from birth to death slab. In the face of television and the discotheque it seems that the life of the old cinema tradition has run full cycle and is now back where it started, except that the days of wine and roses are over and it has nothing left to offer or look forward to. With THE EXORCIST in Largs and THE GODFATHER in Glasgow it is no wonder that the morals of our youth are at their lowest ebb.

1977

July 2nd, Saturday

The day after my sixty-fourth birthday. Jane and I set out on our 300 mile journey from Aberdeen to Isle of Whithorn, near the Mull of Galloway, the Land's End of Scotland, where we had previously booked a caravan from a Mrs. C. Johns of 11 James Nesbit Street, Glasgow, for a week. The caravan cost us £30, of which I sent £5 deposit by post on booking, and paid the remaining £25 on arrival, where Mrs. Johns and her husband were waiting for us in the caravan, to give us instruction in the use of the gas cooker, lighting, water and sanitation, etc., and to give us the key, which we were to leave at the reception office on our departure the following Saturday.

It wasn't a new caravan and had been on the site for some time, but Mrs. Johns had just bought it in the spring when we made our booking and she said we were her first tenants. What she didn't know was that her first customer was David Toulmin the novelist and I didn't tell her; better to keep these things quiet and you get more peace. Perhaps she had never heard of me, but after the publicity of BLOWN SEED in the Glasgow newspapers I wouldn't have risked it, especially when Mrs. Johns was so familiar with the people in the next caravan, also from Glasgow.

The journey took us a round of the clock, almost twelve hours from the time we left home at 5.15 a.m. to 4.45 p.m. when we arrived at Burrowhead Caravan Site, including three stops for tea, the last at Crossraguel Abbey, between Ayr and Girvan, where we stayed for an hour to rest and look over the place. But we still had a long way to go, much further than I thought, facing a head wind from the south-west, which tore at the windscreen and swung the car on exposed stretches of the road, a wind battling with rain and so long as it kept up it would remain dry, or so the man at the abbey had said. But such a pleasure these new motorways are, driving straight through everything, without having to divert to such places as Brechin, Stirling, Dunblane, Ayr, Troon, Irvine, Saltcoats, etc., not including small picturesque places like Largs and

Girvan, where it is a pleasure to call and look at the shops. Perth is now the worst bottleneck, being all one-way streets, where I lost myself on the way home, and it will remain so until the new bridge over the Tay is completed to provide a diversion.

Our first impression of the Burrowhead camping site was disappointing: so far away from everything of interest it seemed as we drove further and further down the coast from Glenluce, where we forked right from the main Stranraer-Dumfries road. What had seemed like a mere seven miles on the map now turned out to be seventeen or even 20 miles, owing of course to my own hasty miscalculation. Luce Bay in sunshine is a lovely place (as we later discovered—despite the smell at low tide) but in our present circumstances, after a long and tiring journey, it seemed the most lonely and forlorn place we could have come to; nothing but what we could have seen at home, whins and scree and abundant rock, the grey dismal sea on our right and a curtain of fog encroaching upon us. Places like Chapel Finian and St. Ninian's Cave (sign-posted by the roadside) I passed without interest, although I was aware of their mystic association with our religious tradition, earlier even than our own St. Drostan at Aberdour, or St. Columba on Iona. Villages like Port William and Monreith, quaint and beautiful on the bays, their wind-bent trees overhanging the cliffs, we now practically ignored, so great was our anxiety to reach Isle of Whithorn, which even then was not the end of our journey, having to motor another mile-and-a-half along the desolate cliff tops to Burrowhead.

All day Sunday we stopped in the caravan, engulfed by seeping fog, except for a stroll to the cliff edge to look at the crags. I read all day from David Niven's BRING ON THE EMPTY HORSES, with no interest whatsoever in our intended safari into Bonnie Gallowa'. All around us of course was plenty of noise and people enjoying themselves in physical pursuits: children on the trampoline, swings and chutes and diving into the swimming pool quite near to us, while grown-ups thronged to the shop for provisions and the Sunday papers. During the week the camp-site pub was open, the bingo arcades and the dance hall, where a crescendo of pop music and screaming teenagers persisted till nearly midnight, when they dispersed

168

in noisy jubilation. But on the evening of Sunday it rained; fairly danced on the roof of the caravan, mocking our holiday spirits in heedless derision, until we had thoughts of an early home-going.

On Monday, 4th July light came early but fog so thick we couldn't observe the sea only a few hundred yards distant. However we dressed and had breakfast of bacon and egg and determined to go somewhere in spite of the fog. Around ten o'clock we were in Wigtown, when the sun came out in all his glory, dispersing the fog and throwing his mantle of light upon the unveiling countryside. For the rest of the week he never blinked an eyelid, but blazed down upon us in toasting splendour. And such a pleasant little place is Isle of Whithorn, like an old water-colour out of the past, where some of the houses and the white church are lapped by the water at high tide, though we saw it mostly at low water, with the small yachts and fishing boats of various colours keeled over on their sides in the green bottom of the harbour. Then Whithorn proper with its wide main street bearing downhill to the sea, with the noble church of St. John near the foot of the square, now sheared of its tower and serving as a garage (something which has happened to a great many of our old country churches) where the House of our Lord has become a counting house, selling petrol to the tourists. On either side of the main street are some very old houses with slightly sunken roofs, and in the centre of the village the square clock tower which seems to rise from the roofs of the tenements and is unapproachable from the street front; behind it the old priory, founded by St. Ninian in the fifth century and later dedicated to St. Martin, with the old Parish Church still in use at the far end of the graveyard.

And oh the sweet Bladnoch in its dreamy valley of folded trees, where it flows under the road bridge near the distillery, with a red brick pillar in the middle of the water between the wooded slopes, all that remains of the branch railway from Newton Stewart to Whithorn. Such a wealth of social history these old railway embankments provide, now reclaimed by nature and clothed in her wildest verdure. In Galloway we found rhododendrons on the hillsides, honeysuckle in the hedges, lashings of white sambucus, vermilion maytree, heaven scented hawthorn, giant purple foxgloves, waving oceans of bright red willowherb and pink and white dogrose. When we stopped to pluck the wild honeysuckle the white variety had no smell at all and the red only a little, while the sambucus elder was obnoxious, something of ancient decay and burning compost. It was growing in profusion around the old parish kirk of Kirkinner, an old-fashioned building in pastel shade sandstone with a most becoming interior, enlightened by two windows of stained glass depicting our Lord as The Good Shepherd, family dedications of the neighbourhood. In the heat of the day it was blissfully cool inside the church, and while Jane rested in a pew I read from the minister's Bible, from Psalm 139 "O Lord thou hast searched me and known me. Thou knowest my downsitting and mine uprising, thou understandest my thoughts afar off. . . . My substance was not hid from thee, when I was made in secret, and curiously wrought in the lowest parts of the earth". Such generous poetry is food and drink for my famished soul, and I thank and bless and kiss the hand that wrote it for our wellbeing. Outside in the church-yard was a very old tomb with rambler roses growing inside the rusted railings. I took a photograph of the old kirk before we left though Jane declined from standing among the gravestones.

The whole peninsula of Wigtownshire reminds me of the Black Isle, between the firths of Moray and Cromarty; so rich in farming land and browsing cattle, though I believe the herds here are even larger, with some of the newer breeds in evidence, especially the French Charolais and a sprinkling of the German Semmentil. The farms too seem more expansive and their steadings modernised and the latest machinery in use. Breeding cattle are plentiful but the dairy herds predominate, comprising the popular Ayrshire-Friesian bigger boned animals. Sheep are less common despite the rough pasture and pigs are a minority, at least in comparison with the north of Scotland.

The farmers were busy with their hay and silage, sometimes handling both crops simultaneously, great wide fields of it, cutting and baling, with clouds of pollen rising from the grass, rich in protein for the winter feeding of cattle. The fog had cleared and we now sweltered in heat, the farmers taking every opportunity to secure their crops, working late in the evenings.

The only disadvantage I observed was the multifarious outcrops of virgin rock in the coastal fields, and some of it well inland, where the modern implements have to be guided round them to secure the grass, which would be even more frustrating and even dangerous with a top-heavy combine harvester in a barley crop, and I remarked to Jane that I certainly wouldn't like to drive a tractor in this sort of terrain.

From our caravan site in the mornings we could now see the Isle of Man, twenty-eight miles away through the haze, but during the afternoons it disappeared completely. On the first day of sunshine we motored through the Galloway Hills, going as far as Pinmore on the Girvan road, where we branched off to Barr and Dalquhairn, following the course of the Stinchar, where I took Jane's photo in midstream, sitting on a rock, while the sun sparkled the waters through a moving pattern of leaves, cool and refreshing to be out of the heat, while the burn babbled his endearing song. We stopped at Barr, with Polmaddie hill in the background, green rolling and edifying behind the red spire of the church above the village. Children were playing in the burn and well dressed old ladies sat on benches in the public park.

We doubled back from Dalquhairn, where there seemed to be the workings of a coalmine, and where I stopped for petrol and enquired about the magnificent castle in the woods, where I asked permission to see it at the lodge, but I was refused, even though it was empty, because of people taking things away the woman said, master's orders, so I had to be content with viewing the castle through binoculars from a vantage point on the road. We had a delightful tea by the roadside, brewed in our flasks from the new perforated tea-bags, ham and tomato sandwiches, scones and sponge cake, while I consulted my map and took my bearings, smoked my pipe and dreamed my dreams, the green fields all round us and the sun shimmering on the hillsides. It was fifty years to the week since I left school and worked on my first farm, and as I gazed around me what changes I beheld, not a man on his feet but all seated on tractors, most of them ignorant of the days of the plodding horse and manual labour; all that was in the past and I had lived to see both sides of the mirror. Most of the men I worked with in those early days are dead; they did not live to see the machines relieve them of their burdens, or some of them only partially, while I have beheld modern farm workers transformed to robots, working only their brains and their hands while we exercised the whole body, so it is no wonder the male human frame is degenerating in stature, and that fewer of them may live to claim their old-age pension.

That first day of our tour we certainly had our fill of the Galloway hills, beautiful but terrifying on the road we took south, following the bed of the Water of Minnoch before it joins the Cree, in the shadow of the Merrick (2764 ft.) and Glentrool forest. It was a knife-edge road with terrifying gullies opening out on either side, first on my right and then on my left going south, but fortunately not simultaneously, especially when we met a cattle float, a van and a car with a caravan on one of the bends, where they halted to let me into a passing recess. Down in the valleys the dry-stone sheep-folds looked like small rings that had slipped from some giant's fingers, the streams like wayward ribbons they had cast over their shoulders. Now and then we had the clatter of a cattle grille, and right on the summit of the road we had to open a gate. But even with this distraction the Galloway Hills were indescribably beautiful, persuading me to stop the car for one of those "once in a lifetime" views, while all around stood those silent giants of the ages: brown and green plush inlaid with jewelled rock, pastelled over with bright sun patch and moving cloud shadow, with purple hollows where the heather was in bloom, their skirts embroidered with mauve rhododendron and bright red foxglove and willow-herb, merging with the trees in the valleys, uplifting the mind in a strange feeling of mystery, probing back through the centuries and the unchangeable, thankful to be there in this fleeting moment of time.

And what can I say of Glentrool—and the beautiful loch lying there so quiet and restful, surrounded by those brown hills with their stoney summits, their pine skirts to the water's edge, the wild goats on their ridges, set against a sky of summer cloud, white as fleeced wool, shadowed loch deep in the blue serenity. On an outcrop of rock stands the Bruce monument, spanning some 600 years of history, where the Scots King gained his second victory over an English force in 1307. To think that men fought and died in the midst of such beauty;

that their being was but a feather in the wind, and we as the children of eternity were allowed to enjoy it in peace.

From here we followed the Cree to Minnigaff and its lovely rose-pink church, tall and graceful in its splendour, like a shaft of brick-dust sunshine in the green folding woods. The Cree too is beautiful where it flows under the old road bridge at Newton Stewart, a stolid structure that has to cope with a heavy volume of traffic from Stranraer to Dumfries, now much increased from Ireland since our joining of the Common Market in Europe. Like its sister towns of Galloway, Newton Stewart is a busy market town with its jostling main street and gay shops selling trinkets and novelties to the tourists admiring its beauty.

At Wigtown we visited the site and graves of the Covenanting Martyrs, where two women, one of 18 and one of 64 were tied to a stake on the salt marches and drowned by the incoming tide, while the two men were hanged without trial in the town, a bloody smirch on the otherwise chivalrous sounding name of Bonnie Dundee of Claverhouse. We walked round the big Parish Church but could find no entry. A lot of churches are locked nowadays because of the vandals, which would otherwise remain open, and even decent lavatories are hard to find because of this prevalent foolishness, and one can only hope that circumstances will backfire on the hooligans themselves in later years when they find themselves and their families in desperation for a convenience. The day was stifling hot and the car upholstery like an oven, so that we sat for a time in the shade of a monumental gravestone in the churchyard. Fortunately the ice-cream in Wigtown was delightful and with several helpings on successive days we managed to keep cool on it.

In midweek we travelled through Gatehouse of Fleet and Creetown to Kirkcudbright, over its scalloped bridge into the centre of the town, where we walked round MacLelland's Castle, and I took Jane's photograph sitting beside the war memorial, a warrior on a pedestal with shield and sword, a despairing child at his feet, facing the High Street. Across the square from the statue is the Roman Catholic Church of Greyfriars, where the local hoodlums had wrenched the money box from the wall, though fortunately they had not defaced the beautiful interior. Round the corner on the harbour front there is a small picture gallery, where we paid 10p. each to look at the paintings, which proved very much worth while, both upstairs and down, especially the floral works in their delicate water-colouring, and some of the landscapes were also quite captivating. The only modern work which interested me was a woodland scene where you could have plucked the fungus bark from the birch trees; superimposed of course with some strange material but very realistic.

By now we had bought and despatched most of our postcards and procured some small gifts for the family; mostly the now almost traditional linen or cotton dish towels with the local scenic views of places visited, which are mostly hung on the walls and seldom used for the purpose they were intended for, though the colours are fast after frequent washing. So there was no anxiety of purchase and Jane could now shop freely in Kirkcudbright, mostly provisions for the caravan. Some men find this boring but I can always find something to interest me while Jane is in the shops, either in the shops themselves with their crafts and pictures, bric-à-brac and books, or in the buildings outside from the pavements and the people in the streets.

Our goal was now Dundrennan Abbey, that vision in stone in the green pastures with the trees just topping the crumbling walls, the high Gothic windows framing the opalescent sky like a psalmist's dream; where angelic voices in holy worship had once echoed in the vaulted ceilings, pillared on groined arch and chiselled rib; a hymnary in stone, edifying even in its desolation, where the strife of centuries is hushed in the lap of time. What pageantry has worn those flagstones? Such cardinal splendour has been here; such mitred pomp, and the hooded monk in slow sequestered meditation. My guide book says the abbey is of Norman design with transitional work, but it is not my aim to give a scholarly description of these old buildings we have visited, all of which has already been done before with more erudite exposition than I could expend upon them.

I have known for a long time however that Mary Queen of Scots spent her last night in Scotland at Dundrennan Abbey, and now that I have witnessed her last refuge I am satisfied. Over the years we have visited every abbey in the south of

174

Scotland, excepting Dryburgh and Roslin, but including Sweetheart Abbey, which we examined some years ago, and Luce Abbey, which we looked at on the present itinerary. We have also seen most of the castles of Galloway, excluding Threave and Kenmure and the Castle of St. John in the centre of Stranraer.

On the day we travelled to Luce Abbey we also looked at Park Castle, which is presently being renovated, and with which the ancient abbey is associated. From here we motored to Castle Kennedy and its fairyland gardens, so extensive and varied, from the giant lily pond to the terraced greens and woodlands and the wide blue lochs on either side, with boating on the waters; and Lochinch Castle on the same estate, though I only had time to look at it through binoculars and was content to buy a postcard view.

By the end of the week we had taken much more kindly to the Burrowhead caravan site, especially when a woman camper reminded us that there were no midges on the site and no flies; no beach smells and plenty of fresh sea breezes, though I did grudge having to carry our water and empty the sewage container, the only consolation in this being that it took my thoughts back nearly 40 years to my days as a youthful cottar on the Buchan farms. During the last two days we had confined ourselves to the Wigtown peninsula, tripping to such places as Whauphill, Mochrum, Kirkcowan, Sorbie and Galiston, where as always the old churches fascinated me, where I seem to find the whole history of the parishes in the graveyards, and if the door is unlocked I will tip-toe inside to read the Hebrew poetry in the divine silence of eternity. At Mochrum church, in the early evening, within sight of the manse, I could see as much through the rather low windows of plain glass I didn't trouble to try the door handle.

By the side of an old bridge over the Tarf Water near Kirkcowan we had our last tea-break in Galloway, on the stone floor of an old cottage by the roadside, where honeysuckle and clematis still twined with the ivy in the hedges, some of which Jane uprooted for propagating at home, preserving the plants in a polythene bag with a drop of water. On our last day on the site we also dug up some thyme from the cliff-tops, and a setting of thrift or sea-pink, which I like to

175

call sea-clover, because of its likeness to the red meadow variety.

I had also by now managed to finish the book I was reading, BRING ON THE EMPTY HORSES, by David Niven, and had bought his other book, THE MOON'S A BALLOON in Kirkcudbright. I know I have read the wrong book first but that doesn't matter. I have had fun combining two of my interests on holiday: cinema lore and the antiquarian.

We started off home early on Saturday morning the 9th July, getting up at 4 a.m. and we were on the road by 6 o'clock, never saying goodbye to anyone because they were still in bed, and we dropped the key of the caravan in the office letter-box. Bonnie Gallowa' was still very much asleep when we purred through the quiet towns, beautiful in their dreams as in their waking hours, the grey lurking sea never far from their door-steps and the blue rolling hills of morning watching over them. We made for New Galloway, where we had to wait thirty minutes for petrol, having motored round the slopes of Craignelder and missed a great deal in our anxiety that we might run out of petrol in this mountainous but beautiful country. From then on to Ayr and Largs and up the shores o' Clyde to Gourock and over the Erskine Bridge to better known territory, including the Lake of Menteith, arriving home safely around 6 p.m., having covered 979 miles and spent around £80—five times more than it would have cost us when I started this book.

July 16th, Saturday

Letter to Dr. Paul Dukes, lecturer in Russian History at King's College, Aberdeen, with whom I have recently become acquainted, and who had so kindly offered us residence in the old manse of Leslie, near Insch, for a week in his absence.

Dear Paul,

We returned from Leslie yesterday, Friday 15th, and today it is raining. But we had a wonderful week and the sun shone most of the time. Thursday was the only day we had to kindle a fire. We had trouble with the 'phone on the first night (Monday, 11th) and couldn't sleep for the ringing of it; nor could I get through to the exchange and there was no peace until I left it off the hook, and even then it purred most of the night like a cat at the foot of the stairs. The women were terrified because they thought someone was trying to frighten us off, and every moment they expected someone at the windows. Next morning I went to the police at Insch, who got in touch with the post-office and they soon sorted things out. Within two hours an engineer rang me from the top of a pole somewhere and said he had just disentangled our 'phone wires from a tree branch and that we should have no more trouble with the receiver. After this we all three of us (Jane, myself and Vera) settled down to a very pleasant and enjoyable stay in the old manse; a friendly, peaceful, companionable place, where one can be secluded without being isolated, sequestered without being lonely; at least that's how we felt, and by the end of the week we had all fallen in love with the place.

My thoughts here have been beautiful, tranquil and nostalgic, going back half-a-century and embracing some of my finest moments in literature. I have had the opportunity of comparing myself with Ruskin at Brantwood, James Thomson (of the Seasons) at Doddington, Carlyle at Chelsea, Southey at Keswick, or even as Tolstoy among his peasants, and I think it wonderful that Kilvert's diaries emerged from such environment as I find here, and that I can associate my thoughts with Goldsmith and THE VICAR OF WAKEFIELD, the Brontës, George Crabbe and a host of classical writers.

What I have found in your library is not so much a choice of the books I like but an opportunity to examine those I wasn't sure about, and to express an opinion on them, which I am afraid must be unfavourable, like the Wessex Poems of Thomas Hardy and those of Dylan Thomas, including UNDER MILK-WOOD: Hardy being too reminiscent of Swinburne and Thomas an intoxicated juggler with words, most of which I previously suspected but am now convinced. I do not have the time or the inclination to unravel these riddles in poetry and I'm doubtful if the drunken Welshman understood them himself, or if they are merely the product of an unbalanced lunacy, not to be compared with the rational melancholy of Blake or Cowper. I may be simple minded but I still prefer the melody of Tennyson or Longfellow, Campbell or Andrew Lang, or even the grave gay rhapsody of W. H. Davies, where I came across

the following from THE SONG OF LIFE, which I should like to
adopt as my philosophy in later years:

"If I can pluck the rose of sunset, or
The moon's pale lily, and distil their flower
Into one mental drop to scent my soul
I'll envy no man his more worldly power."

I have also had the chance to glance at the works of Henry
Fielding and some of the lesser Elizabethan dramatists; not the
poets, who are already familiar to me. I have spent my time
between scything the glebe and the Scythian Shepherds of
Marlowe's Tamburlaine, though the euphonical connection
confounds me, like the presence of Persephone in the Garioch.
Christopher Marlowe I have so far neglected, partly in favour
of Shakespeare but mostly through my preoccupation with the
cinema, which after all was the theatre of my youth, the visual
poetry of my age. But oh how I revel in the skeleton shaking
themes of those rhetoric bards, and only in these and in the
pastoral qualities of the bible can my emancipated mind now
find repose and inspiration. But it is too late in life for me to
study the serious poets as a student and I must take them solely
for pleasure. But the elegant mind can identify with the
farmyard, as witness this gem from Fielding's PASQUIN:

"Sense is the parent still of fear; the fox,
Wise beast, who knows the treachery of men,
Flies their society, and skulks in woods,
While the poor goose in happiness and ease,
Fearless grows fat within its narrow coop,
And thinks the hand that feeds it is a friend,
Then yield thee, common-sense, nor rashly dare
Try a vain combat against superior force."

The moral here my friend has a double meaning, for if the
poor goose left his coop he might become the prey of the
marauding fox, so it is difficult to say which is the best society
for animals, nature or humanity; at least humanity kills
humanely while nature is brutal and painful.

For most of my rustic life I have scribbled in cottar houses,
with few books to hand from which to cull my thoughts. This
is the first time I have ever written in the sanctum of a Manse,
at a proper roll-top desk, with the classics of literature peering

down at me, and as the years pass another of my ambitions have been fulfilled. And when I think of the "Sternes" and "Spurgeons" who have lived here, all those years ago, and the many sermons they have composed, I feel I am in jocund company.

It is now midnight and the women have gone to bed, blackness at the windows and the creak of floorboards under my stockinged feet, waiting for the ghosts of yesteryear. . . .

Wednesday. Jane would make a fine minister's wife, calling me for tea from the dingle, and I have thoughts of Milton's "When the mower whets his scythe". In the afternoon I walked about on stilts and provoked her to gales of laughter. Even widowed Vera was forced to smile, to laugh out loud, who had lately set her grief upon a monument, but now her tears of laughter were glistening on her cheeks. Her husband Archibald died last summer of cancer, that had formerly been my brother-in-law and friend, my comforter in despair, adviser and nearer brother than in-law.

We all had a wonderful time at Leslie and we hereby thank you sincerely for your generosity in allowing us the privilege of tenancy. I have tidied up the place as best I could and it was a pleasure dividing my time between the garden and your study, which after all has been my life style these fifty years or so. I have taken the liberty of "borrowing" your Marlowe and W. H. Davies, and also a dozen of your 78 r.p.m. records, all of which will be returned to you in due course. I trust you find everything else as you left it and we paid the few 'phone calls we made.

I (we) hope you have had a good spell at Croydon and that Rosie and the children are well and happy. We had a wonderful time in Galloway and I still have to give account of it in my Book of Memory, which you may read later.

I came across the following in W. H. Davies which I think would be an apt introduction for your latest book OCTOBER AND THE WORLD, unless I have a wrong conception of its contents:

> "Fools that we are to think of fame, when there's a force
> To make a coffin of this world of ours
> And sweep it clean of every living thing—
> What then becomes of man and all his powers?"

Davies survived to the fringe of the nuclear age and he may have forseen its "grave" danger. Or he may have written it from the simple fear of God. But God in man has now become more manifest—now that he has the power to destroy himself, which also gives him the privilege of saving himself, if he is wise. This was all he needed to make him God, the first step in complete fulfilment, and the peace of a thousand years.

Best Wishes,

David Toulmin